Free Your Soul

Free Your Soul

Five Keys to Finding Peace in the Storms of Life

My amazing and special Lisa,
   You are one of the most beautiful soul's that I have had the honor to encounter in my lifetime. It is time for you to honor that beauty, put yourself first and become your own soulmate.

YANIRA CRESPO

Love Yourself!

Love,
Yanira Crespo

This is a work of creative nonfiction. The events are portrayed to the best of the author's memory. While all the stories in this book are true, some names and identifying details have been changed to protect the privacy of the people involved.
ISBN: 1535366508
ISBN 13: 9781535366502

This book is dedicated to all of my family, friends, healers, and spiritual teachers who have helped me through my journey towards healing and discovering inner peace.

Introduction

FOR MANY YEARS I studied psychology, and religion, read hundreds of self-help books, went through traditional therapy, and yet I couldn't find peace in my soul no matter what I tried. I endured years of suffering until I finally discovered the tools I needed to heal my pain. After reaching deep levels of peace in my soul, I was inspired to help others find this level of peace within themselves. Allow me to guide you in reaching the inner peace you have been searching for yet haven't found. Let me help you free your soul from the shackles of pain and suffering and guide you to finding true inner peace.

Peace and joy can be found while you are in the midst of the storm. I will provide you with the tools to help--exercises and meditations. There are no coincidences; if you have been drawn to read the pages in this book, then you are ready to heal and let go of what no longer serves you and holds you back from achieving peace in your soul.

Throughout my own journey I discovered valuable tools and healing modalities that created tremendous healing and peace. Having to overcome my own darkness has led me to help others. I understand what it's like to be in a deep depression and not see a way out. I understand how challenging it is to see the light when you're consumed in deep darkness. I understand the devastation of having my world fall apart everywhere

I turned. I experienced an abusive childhood that created deep-rooted wounds which kept me from seeing my worth and from loving myself. These wounds led to marrying young in search of the father I never had and a fairytale family life that didn't exist. The marriage eventually ended and I was left emotionally and mentally bankrupt to raise my two sons on my own. The unhealed wounds and pain I was carrying created a debilitating illness that kept me bedridden and in a wheel chair for a year. Poverty kept me struggling both physically and mentally to make ends meet; we barely had enough to survive. As if all of this were not enough, I watched my aunt suffer through cancer and paralysis as she slowly disintegrated for twenty years until her death. My twenty-nine year old cousin tragically and unexpectedly passed away, leaving a major void in my heart and in my family. I had believed all of this was the worst pain I could experience until my son became very ill. Then I discovered the most pain parents can experience besides burying their child is witnessing their suffering. For years I endured watching my son experience deep pain and there was nothing I could do. When I finally reached a point in my life where I was living the life of my dreams, I lost it all. I had to endure the pain of the loss of a life I once loved and enjoyed.

As horrible as these painful and traumatic events were, I discovered they were all here to help me--not hurt me. Once I understood the reason these painful events had occurred, I was able to find peace. The pain and suffering were here to show me the parts of myself that needed healing. These events were mirroring in me what I couldn't see otherwise. My outer world was a mere reflection of my inner world.

I learned that everything and everyone was here to mirror me in some way or another. Everything was *for* me and not against me. It was also very healing when I no longer pointed a finger and became accountable for my own happiness. It was freeing when I no longer held anyone responsible for my emotional and mental state. A big shift in my life was created when I began to see every encounter as an opportunity to witness the healing that was seeking to be healed. The universe was constantly speaking to me; I just needed to be still and listen. As I continued to ask the universe to show me the reason why someone or something was showing up in my life in a negative way, the answers came. The universe reflected back the reasons people were showing up in the ways they were. Once the answer came, the person or experience no longer had to show up for me in that way.

Once I grasped the truth of all of this, I was able to find peace with everything that happened to me. Nothing was against me it was all for me and was happening for my greater good and my deepest healing. My soul was calling to be healed and the suffering inspired me to seek relief. The most valuable lesson I learned is that even though we come to learn, heal, and grow, the ultimate goal is to experience unconditional love of self and of others. Love heals everything. Love solves everything. Love is everything!

Once I was ready to heal everything, all I was in need of began to emerge. I was led to the right spiritual teachers, healers, coaches, books, and healing modalities. It was through my spiritual healing journey that I learned about the contracts we create before embarking on our trip to earth. Our soul comes to earth to learn lessons, balance karma, and heal past lives. We choose painful events that will teach us what we need to learn, in turn creating the growth that our soul needs in order to evolve. To accomplish what we came to do, we must choose our parents, spouses, lovers, friends, children, family members, and events to help us heal and teach us what we need to learn. Also, what we didn't master in previous lifetimes, we try to master in our present life. I learned that all the events and painful experiences I attracted were mirroring what was calling to be healed.

This understanding helped me get through those painful experiences with greater ease. As I continued to experience the pain, I was able to identify which parts of my wounds were healed and the parts that weren't healed. I saw the losses as awakening moments that were leading me to bigger and better potential in myself. I was being lifted to greater heights. I shed the parts of myself that no longer were serving me and rose to higher vibrations that would bring forth more positive experiences.

"In every tragedy a blessing is born"

When I was able to heal the darkness in me (shadow self), I finally tapped in to the inner light that was already there. Having to go within is not an easy task. It can be very scary. Facing your emotions and yourself can take its toll. As humans we believe we are afraid of facing our own darkness…when in reality we are afraid of our divine light. Our light is more powerful than any inner darkness we may carry. It's our own power that scares us to look within. We fear our light. However, once we tap into that light within we no longer fear it, but embrace it as our true selves. Our divine selves. Who we *really* are. In the darkest moments of our lives is when our soul transforms the most. It's difficult to see the light in those challenging times, but in these moments that's when one must have faith in the light that is shining through.

Through my own healing journey, I began to feel a deep love and desire to share this awareness with humanity. I now experience a peace and joy I never knew possible. I discovered five essential keys to healing that helped me release my pain and create the relief I needed, and now I want to share them with you.

"Pull the root of pain, plant the seed of healing, and the soul will blossom"

Key 1

Powerful Prayers and Meditation

B ELIEVING IN A power greater than your own can lead to tremendous peace. Talking to God/Higher Power/angels and asking for healing is a true gateway to a peaceful soul. As a child I had no one to talk to and I did not feel any support from my family. I struggled with friendships, and quite frankly, felt alone. What helped me get through the painful experiences in my life were my conversations with God and my faith. I always believed that God was there for me. He would never abandon me even though everyone else did. He was my best friend. My mother always said I was born knowing the existence of God. When we pray we invite the love and light of our higher power into our souls. We are surrounded by angels and guides just waiting for us to ask for help.

I began to experience an even stronger connection to the spirit world at five years old. I remember sitting in the back seat of my mother's car, and felt someone tapping my shoulder. When I looked, there was no one there. Sleep was always a challenge for me, because I would feel people in my room, even lying on my bed, but I couldn't see anyone there. I used to see and hear things that others didn't see or hear. I would have these intense and scary dreams that made no sense and would wake me up in a sweat. There were times I felt complete terror as I was surrounded by spirits that looked and felt evil. It wasn't until my adult years that I learned about my intuitive gifts. Once I discovered my connection to the spirit world I began to understand myself more and my life's purpose and mission.

As I grew older, my connection and communication with spirits and the angels grew stronger. I was able to provide messages from deceased loved ones, the angels, and spirit guides to those in need. I would have visions and dreams that were divine messages too. My ability to hear and see them became clearer. It was fascinating to discover angels and how they are a healing force in our lives. Everyone who received these messages was amazed by the accuracy and healing effect. People would express how much lighter they felt in my presence as if a weight were lifted. Many felt they were in the presence of an angel and that God was speaking to them through me. Through the years my gift continued to grow and evolve. I was able to see past lives that were affecting people in their current lives. I used this information to help them heal that past lifetime, which healed their present lifetime. Seeing how my gift was helping people heal inspired me to continue using my divine connection to help those who were in need.

I also discovered I had the ability to feel other people's pain. I didn't understand why I was feeling those around me, and I struggled with these feelings and emotions. It was not until I became an adult that I learned this sensitivity was due to being an empath. Even though it's challenging to have this ability, it helps me understand people at a deeper level. This ability helps tremendously when I'm working as a facilitator in my healing practice. However, I have to use special prayers and protection tools to manage my empath abilities or it can be quite overwhelming for me.

My passion to help others led me to a healing modality that would enhance my connection with the angels. Integrated Energy Therapy taps into the energy of the divine angels and removes the trauma from our energy fields, and integrates the healing energy of the angels. When I began to incorporate this new healing modality into my healing practice, the results were astonishing. With the assistance of the angels and guides, I am able to tap into people's subconscious mind to see what needs healing. I'm able to tap into everything the person needs to heal as the angels are guiding me. What's more, when I discovered the Akashic Records, my ability to tap into the deep parts of the person's soul that needs attention, love, and healing were enhanced. The Akashic Records are our book of life: everything that is stored in our DNA. When combining both Integrated Energy Therapy along with the Akashic Records, the person experiences deep healing and transformation.

Through my own personal experiences and the experiences of all the people I have helped, there is great power in the power of prayer. No matter what you are experiencing in life--good or challenging-- pray for help. There is an army of angels, deceased loved ones, and Ascended Masters waiting to assist you. All you have to do is ask.

Call on these angels in the moments you need help.

ANGELS OF HEALING

Cassiel— heals heartache, emptiness, longing, grief, abandonment, loss, and betrayal.

Azarael— helps assist souls as they transition to heaven and the loved ones who are left to grieve.

Daniel— heals anger, resentment, bitterness, judgment, and hatred over past wrongs and fills you with forgiveness.

Ariel— helps you overcome your limitations and live your life's purpose.

Rafael— helps you heal pain and when you are feeling alone, are losing hope, feel abandoned, or are struggling to find God/Higher Power/Source.

Gabriel— helps you with communication and when you feel uncertain about your life's path, and fills you with trust.

Celestina— helps you when you're afraid of what others may think of your creativity by giving you confidence.

Faith— helps you when you're losing hope by filling you with faith.

Sarah— helps you overcome feelings of powerlessness and stress by empowering you.

Michael— helps you overcome fear by helping you feel safe and giving you courage.

Metatron— helps those who are highly sensitive and gifted. If you have special gifts that require being medicated or have challenges adjusting to society, He can help you.

You'll notice significant changes in your emotions, thoughts, and well-being when you call upon God/Higher Power and the angels for help. You'll notice that the levels of stress diminish, and you'll become a more calm and centered person. Talk to them as if you were talking to a close friend.

There are specific prayers that I use when needing to find immediate healing and peace or when I want to manifest something quickly. I'll share some examples of the prayers I used when wanting to manifest my heart's desires. Keep in mind everything has a divine timing. Just because you haven't seen the answer to your prayers, it doesn't mean the prayer will not be answered. If what you're asking for is for your higher good, and it's in the divine plan for you, it will be answered. You can use these prayers as a guideline and complete the words to align with your needs.

PRAYERS

"I call in God, the Angels, Ascended Masters, deceased loved ones and my entire spiritual team. Fill my spirit with the peace that only you can give. Help me see with the spiritual eye and reach acceptance of what is now. I declare and know now that my _____ will heal and thrive. Thank you for gifting me a happy and healthy ____. I surrender the outcome to you. I let go and let God. And so it is!"

"Dear God and the Angels I declare and know that the perfect ___ for me is mine now. Thank you for gifting me with the ___ that brings me joy and abundance. I release. I let go and let God. Amen!"

"God, you promised to give me the secret desires of my heart. Today I remind you of _____ that my soul deeply desires. Thank you for blessing me with _____. I thank you for _____. And so it is!"

These prayers have been very powerful for me and for those with whom I have shared them. Prayer helps us build our faith and sustain it through the most turbulent times in our lives. Faith is believing in what we can't yet see. If we can focus on a positive outcome and not on the painful experience, we will find acceptance and peace. Believe no matter what the situation looks like, God is in control leading you to healing and restoration. These painful experiences are God's way of raising us to higher levels we never would reach otherwise. The soul's greatest evolution is reached through the deepest pain. It's in the pain that we learn, grow, mature, and become stronger. If you can see the storms as blessings in disguise, you'll reach acceptance--which leads to being the calm in the storm.

The universe is constantly communicating with us, giving us signs to guide us towards our divine destiny. It's important to stay open and be aware of the signs. You can ask for specific signs you need and the universe will respond. One of the ways that the angels communicate with us is through numbers. When they sense we need help they will show us specific numbers that have special meanings. When I used to feel fear I would see the number 444. When I saw this sequence in numbers I knew the angels were telling me that I had nothing to fear.

When I felt unsupported I would see the number 333, which meant the Ascended Masters were with me. When I was being negative or was trying to manifest something into my life, I would see 111, which means to keep my thoughts positive. Usually I tell people to make a wish when they see this number, because our wishes are truly our heart's desires. In the moments when I lost my faith in humanity, 222 would show up to remind me not to lose the faith. There is a free website called Joanne Sacred Scribes: (http://sacredscribesangelnumbers. blogspot.com/). Here you will find all the number sequences and their meanings. I recommend you visit this site as it will be a great resource in understanding the sacred meaning of these numbers. Also, Doreen Virtue has a booked called *Angel Numbers 101* which has all the angel number meanings.

When my son was going through a very difficult time and experienced several hospitalizations, I started believing that rainbows were coming. Even though at the moment all we saw were clouds…I believed. A month after I started declaring the rainbows were coming, things began to change in my son. A deep strength began to form inside of him and a strong desire to heal emerged. He even saw rainbows outside his hospital room. Before I knew it the clouds lifted and the rainbows came with sunshine and blue skies. No matter what you're going through always believe the storm will pass and blessings will come.

Meditations are another great source for immediate healing and peace. Praying is *talking* to God, while meditation is *listening* to God. Through meditation you can quiet the mind enough to hear your inner voice and receive messages from the Divine. Much peace and wisdom can be found through meditation. There are many types of meditation and you will have to find the one that works for you. Transcendental

Meditation has been life changing for both my son and me. It helps you tap into your pure consciousness-which alleviates the stress in your mind and body. You are able to connect to deep parts of yourself and heal stored trauma. If you suffer from anxiety, high levels of stress, and are experiencing a painful event in your life, this meditation can be a powerful tool for you. Everyone has different results with this meditation, but for my son and me, it completely eliminated our anxiety and our stress levels. This meditation has many mental, emotional, and physical benefits. Those who suffer from heart disease, diabetes, addictions, as well as other health issues, have benefited greatly from Transcendental Meditation. If you are interested in finding out more about this valuable tool, I recommend you visit www.tm.org and find a center near you.

However, if you are not able to incorporate Transcendental Meditation into your life, you can find several guided meditations on YouTube that can help calm your mind and soul. There are several meditation CDs available too. Find the one that resonates with you and incorporate it into your daily life. Deepak Chopra is very well known for his work in helping people with his meditation techniques. Before I discovered Transcendental Meditation, I listened to all of his CDs, which were helpful.

One of the meditations that I'm sharing with you has helped my clients who suffer from anxiety and experience stress. This meditation has helped them feel immediate calmness. Not only will you experience emotional healing but also physical healing. When we calm our minds, a message is sent to our nervous system to slow down so physical healing can occur. With meditation you benefit mentally, emotionally, and physically.

To listen to the *Healing Meditation* visit https://soundcloud.com/ user-668573947/heart-meditation. However, I recommend you review the written version before listening to the audio.

HEALING MEDITATION

Before starting this meditation:

(Optional yet recommended)

- Allow yourself a few minutes.
- Find a quiet place and time when you will not be interrupted.
- Light a couple of white candles.
- Play calming music in the background, preferably with no lyrics.

Close your eyes, and place both of your hands on your heart. Breathe in and out through your mouth three times. Think of something or someone whom you love unconditionally and are grateful for. Allow yourself to feel that love and gratitude all through your body. Imagine a beam of white light entering your heart, filling up all the voids, and healing all the wounds one by one. Stay in that moment for as long as you feel full.

PRAYER

With both hands still placed on your heart, say the following prayer:

"God, Angels, Masters, and Guides, bring healing to my heart. Help me to see my pain as a gift of learning. Fill my heart with the love and peace that only you can give. Help me find clarity in what I don't understand and accept what I cannot change. Give me courage to face my pain and surround me with your white healing light."

VISUALIZATION

As you ask in prayer to be surrounded by the white light, visualize yourself in a circle of white. This circle of light is very strong that no negativity can enter it. Bask in that light and allow all of this healing energy to enter your body.

This meditation can lead you towards healing any wounds that are creating blocks in your life and keep you living in despair. Yet it's only one tool to healing. Healing is a journey that cannot be done alone. There are many aspects to our healing process that we can't see while we're in our grieving moments. That is why it is very important to seek help and support through these difficult times. It's not time that heals; it's what we do in that time to create that healing.

"Embrace hardships as they lead you to growth, transformation, and a better you."

Key 2

Forgiveness

THE FIRST AND most important part of our healing is forgiveness. In order to set our soul free we must forgive those who have hurt us. Forgiveness comes in many layers, and we must navigate through those layers and forgive each person and event that caused us pain. When we don't forgive, we carry anger and resentment, which steals our peace and creates unnecessary stress, which sickens our body. When we allow people to upset us, we're giving them power over our life. They're in control because we're letting them control our emotions.

People who hurt others are hurt themselves. They don't know how to channel those negative emotions and they release them by lashing out at others. When we start to understand why people do hurtful things, then we can see them with compassion, understanding, and love. This allows our anger and resentment to transform, and we are able to forgive them. No one and nothing is here to hurt us. Every person or experience is here to heal us. There is no wrong in anyone's behavior as he or she is merely showing up in the ways others need. How else will we see our wounds? Everything and everyone is mirroring and triggering our inner wounds that are calling to be healed.

I have always had immense compassion for people who murder, abuse, commit crimes, and do what the world calls horrible behavior. They chose to volunteer to be the so-called "bad" people and sacrifice their lives in order to help others heal. They are judged, incarcerated, killed, and rejected by the world, when they merely are triggering wounds that need healing either from this life or past lives. The pain they "seem" to cause is only the pain that was dormant in others crying to be healed.

When we struggle to forgive ourselves for hurting others or making bad choices, it's because we're not allowing ourselves to be human. We're expecting perfection in ourselves, and we tend to beat ourselves up and become angry with ourselves. Keep in mind when you hurt others you are showing up for them the way they need for their own healing. You are showing them through your so- called "bad" or "hurtful" behavior what their spirit needs to heal.

The first five years of my life were blissful. Even though my mother became pregnant out of wedlock, her fears didn't stop her from having me. She lived off of welfare for the first three years of my life. To make ends meet she took care of her landlord's children until she was ready to go back to work. When I was three years old, she met a wonderful man that became her husband. He stuck around for two years and it was a happy time in our lives. However, he left our lives suddenly and with no explanation. My mother never understood why, but she gracefully accepted the reality of being alone.

A year after my mother's husband left, a man from her past resurfaced. She accepted him back in her life because she believed he had changed. There began my painful journey. From the age of five to sixteen I experienced emotional, mental, and physical abuse. I watched how he constantly mistreated my mother and disrespected her in every way. He always had several women, and was constantly drunk, or high on some drug. Some days he became very violent and dangerous. He would release his anger daily by breaking furniture, TV's, plates, and anything he got his hands on. Other days my mother would be the target and get caught in the crossfire of his violence. Sometimes it would be me. I lived in constant terror. My home was not safe. I never knew how he would react to things and we all walked on eggshells around him. Police officers were constant visitors in our home.

His greed for money led him to burning down several of his businesses. He didn't care if people could possibly die in these fires. All he cared about was collecting money from his insurance policy. This greed for money also led him to drug trafficking and drug addiction. He eventually paid for those crimes and was sentenced several times. When my family became aware of the person my mother was involved with, they did everything in their power to try to help her leave him. However, she denied their help and stayed.

I grew up feeling a lot of anger and resentment towards my parents. It was very painful having a mother who allowed my suffering. In the eyes of a child, all I could see was her love for him and not for me. I felt she chose him over me and he was more important to her. I couldn't understand how a mother could allow anyone to hurt her child. I was angry at her for neglecting my needs. There were times I even suffered from hunger. Even though my parents owned several groceries stores, there was never enough food in the house. I was left home alone most of the time and had to fend for myself. Sometimes my mother would leave me in the care of my stepfather but it was like being alone. He would leave me home alone to go off with his mistress. I remember being only five years old and out of hunger and desperation, cooked my first batch of eggs. At the time I was proud of myself for that accomplishment, but when I look back I see how dangerous that was. Not only could I have burned myself cooking, I could have hurt myself in many other ways. There were other times I was left in his care only to be molested by him. He would be drunk and high on cocaine, and would touch me inappropriately. At the time I didn't know what he was doing, but it didn't feel right to me. I felt very uncomfortable and sad. Even though I didn't understand what was happening to me, I knew it was wrong. I didn't tell my mother because I was too young to articulate what was happening to me.

I grew up being told I was stupid, ugly, and not worth anything. When I didn't comply with his requests, I would be physically attacked, or beaten down with hurtful words. I lived in constant fear and pain. I wasn't even allowed to have any friends or a social life. I was expected to cook and clean every day after school. When my stepfather decided laundry needed to be done, he would dump all the clothes into the bathtub to be hand washed by me. Sometimes it would be up to five loads. We didn't have a dryer, and I had to hang them to dry too! To top it off, at the age of nine, when my brother was born, I became the babysitter. I loved my brother dearly, and he brought a lot of joy to my heart, but no nine year old should have that responsibility.

These difficult circumstances I was living in led to a deep depression. My school performance suffered and I had no hope for a better life. My first suicide attempt was at the tender age of nine. There were two more attempts that followed at the age of fifteen and nineteen. I did find some moments of relief when family members would temporarily take me in to live with them.

I grew up with a suitcase in my hand, feeling like an orphan with no stable home. I had no one to protect me or show me love. I rarely received hugs or love throughout my childhood. My mother was too consumed in her own pain to even notice mine.

These experiences created deep wounds that I would carry for many years. I knew the only way to heal those wounds, and find peace, would be through forgiveness. As I did the inner work, by allowing myself to forgive them, I not only found my peace but I found my truth.

I was able to forgive my mother when I felt compassion for her own pain. Her lack of awareness didn't allow her to see her abusive relationship. I finally understood she was doing the best she could with the awareness she had at the time. She was being manipulated and degraded. The way he treated her made her feel unworthy, unlovable, and just plain stupid. She believed she couldn't survive without him and would fail in life if she left him. All he had to do was plead to her on his hands and knees, cry like a baby, begging her to return. She would feel sorry for him and would cave. When I was older, and heard about his traumatic childhood story, I understood her pity for him. As a child he grew up on a farm. He was known to be very sensitive and emotional. His father didn't understand him and bullied him. He was beaten and picked on for being a crybaby. His mother couldn't deal with watching her son suffer and didn't know how to handle him. When he turned sixteen he was sent to the United States to live with family he had never met. Just like his family on the farm; they rejected him too.

He didn't even know how to speak English. Several times he got lost in the city trying to find his way to work and back home. He never received love or acceptance from any one, not even his own mother. He slept around with several women seeking the love and acceptance he never received as a child. Knowing all of this didn't justify his behavior, but now I understood the reason for the behavior. This understanding led to feelings of compassion for his pain. I saw how my mother only added to his pain by her coldness towards him. I recognized her responsibility in that relationship too.

My mother grew up with parents who did not express love. There were nine children and my grandmother was too busy to be nurturing towards her children. She was too busy working on the farm trying to help my grandfather make ends meet. They were very poor and survived off very little. They lived in a shack and all the children had to walk miles barefoot. They didn't even have enough money to buy their children shoes. My mother had a brother who was very defiant. He was very hyper and misbehaved a lot. In these current times he would be labeled ADHD (Attention Deficit Hyperactivity Disorder) and prescribed medications. However, in those times they were beaten until submission. This really affected my mother greatly and left a deep wound in her. She also had a younger brother who at the tender age of two tragically passed away. The children were outside playing when the young boy fell and hit his head. He was taken to see a doctor and my grandfather came back with him in a coffin. By the time she was twelve she had to leave her parents' home and live with her aunt. Her parents couldn't support her anymore and had to send her away. When she turned eighteen she moved to the United States to live with her older sister. There she worked and was able to support herself. By the time she turned twenty-four she met my biological father who abandoned her and was left to raise me on my own. A few years later she met this amazing man who treated us like gold. They married but he left her two years later. Again, she was abandoned without any explanation and was left heartbroken. Soon after my stepfather came into the picture and she welcomed him with open arms. Deep down she was seeking love and acceptance. That's exactly what my stepfather gave her. He loved my mother with all he had, but my mother didn't know how to return the love. She didn't know how to show her love and this affected my stepfather greatly. He was in desperate need of love since his mother had abandoned him. Since my mother didn't fulfill this need, he sought it out in other women.

All this awareness helped me see them as hurt beings. This was when I was able to feel compassion for their pain. This newfound way of viewing their pain, helped me heal my own. Also, I began to see everything I learned from their mistakes, and the positive things they contributed to my life. I listed the things they did right verses all their wrongs. Now I see there are no mistakes in life. Everything is here to teach us and help us grow. Every experience has a reason and a divine purpose. All was chosen before embarking on our earth journey, but we forget while we are here living the journey. A big part of the journey is to remember why we chose our journey in the beginning. I began to remember how I chose to learn to love myself unconditionally and to accept myself with all my flaws. I discovered my lesson was to learn to see myself only with love.

My mother always accepted me for who I am. She allowed me to be my authentic self. She never questioned or doubted my decisions because she believed in me. She gave me independence and allowed me to fly. She never held me back from achieving anything I wanted.

My stepfather was a very hard-working man. He had a knack for attracting an abundance of money and was great at creating businesses.

These traits taught me to be responsible, to never give up, and go after my dreams. When I married at the young age of nineteen, I already knew how to take care of a household. Even though it was difficult cooking, cleaning, and babysitting as a child, these skills prepared me for marriage. Having to work hard in the home, and work outside the home early in life, prepared me for what was ahead. I owe my strength, determination, courage, and resourcefulness to him. Having to constantly face him and stand up to him, taught me to stand up for what I believed in and not to be afraid of anyone.

Today my mother lives with me and is a great support system. Even though I had to cut all ties with my stepfather, I no longer feel hurt or anger towards him. I genuinely wish him well. I was able to find peace with my painful childhood. I realize now that there truly is nothing to forgive. As every experience is here to teach us what we need to grow. There truly is no wrong or right behavior. Every person and every experience are both here to mirror the parts of ourselves that need healing and love. I realize now that I chose in my soul contract my stepfather to be exactly as he is. I came to learn complete unconditional love and acceptance of myself.

For some of you it's difficult to see the good in others, especially when their imperfect parts are more evident. If you can allow yourself to see the people who hurt you, through the eyes of God, then you open the door to your own healing. Through my painful childhood, I also carried the pain of my biological father's absence from my life. Throughout most of my life I would have nightmares about his lack of existence in my life. At every wedding I would cry as I watched the daughters dance with their fathers. I always knew I wouldn't have my own father to dance with at my wedding. I would never be daddy's little girl. I had to accept that reality, and find healing through forgiveness.

I was able to forgive him when I realized he had nothing positive to contribute to my life. He was a musician with no stability. I would have experienced his abandonment over and over again as he chose his music over me. He was never there for any of his children. I realized I wasn't the problem--he was. His lack of parenting no longer determined my being important, worthy and lovable.

As I worked through the layers of all the pain he caused me, I was finally able to free my soul. This freedom led to reconciling with him and meeting his side of the family. They welcomed me with open arms and hearts filled with love. However, as I began to learn more about this new-found family, I realized all the drama that came with them. Rather quickly I came to the realization that I was better off without them. I was actually spared a lot of heartache from not having them in my life. I made the decision to let go of my father and the family that came with him. But in the time I shared with my father and new-found family, I learned a lot about him. His father had abandoned him and he was raised by his mother. Since they were very poor he had to work at a very early age. He was responsible for supporting his mother and sister. In his early twenties his mother passed away from cancer. His sister had a nervous breakdown and was hospitalized for several months. When he met my mother he was barely making ends meet while my mother had her life together. He felt inferior and believed she deserved better. That's why he decided it was best for them to end their relationship. He moved on to other relationships that never ended well and he has never been there for any of his children.

Today he carries a lot of guilt for his lack of parenting. He gets very attached to his pets as they represent his children. Devoting himself to taking care of his dogs gave him the comfort of not being able to take care of any of his children. His anxiety has only become worse as he continues to carry a lot of guilt over the decisions he's made in his life. I have deep compassion for my father and if he hadn't expected me to be his nurse, I would definitely have him in my life. I have accepted that my life is better without him and I don't need a father to be happy. As much as I would have loved having a father who was loving and supportive, he would never be able to offer what he doesn't carry within himself.

Even though I have that awareness now, I didn't see things with such clarity in my younger years. I was a young woman who craved love, support, and stability. I began seeking religion as a way of receiving what I was lacking at home. In that exploration I found the religion that was right for me. In this religion I discovered I could have a healthy and happy family life. It was there I met the man who was going to become my husband and father of my children. I believed marriage would provide me everything I had lacked growing up. I tried fulfilling my needs by marrying young. I craved desperately to create a healthy/happy home life. I believed I made a wise choice by marrying a man from the church. He had a great reputation and shared the same beliefs. I fell in love and married him with the best intentions. Eight years after the marriage, and two children later, I realized I married for all the wrong reasons. I was seeking someone to fill my voids, heal me, and make me happy. I became aware that we both married for the same reasons, and in order to make our marriage work, we needed to do the "inner work." Our wounded inner childs were running the relationship. We both needed to heal our traumatic childhood wounds. We needed to learn to love ourselves and see our own worth. I was willing to do the work, but he resisted seeking help. When I looked into the sad eyes of my children, my heart yearned for their happiness. I knew if I stayed in this marriage, I could never give them what they deserved. I ended the marriage and there began the "real" inner work.

It took six years after our break up to realize all the anger and resentment I was carrying around. I blamed him for everything, and wasn't taking any responsibility for my part in the marriage. Not only did I have to forgive him for what I perceived as mental/emotional abuse; I had to forgive myself.

When I had the awareness that I attracted this man from my wounded self, then I was able to finally forgive him. Our wounded inner childs were running the show the entire marriage. There were no adults present in that marriage. How could he love and accept me, if I couldn't love and accept myself? How could he see my worth if I couldn't see my own? How could he be kind and encouraging, if I wasn't to myself? This awareness led me to feeling compassion for him and for myself. We were doing the best we could with what we knew at the time. I realized he couldn't save me or make me happy. I had to save myself and find my own happiness. I recognized that being married to this man was a blessing. It led me to discover the wounds that needed healing. I began the journey towards learning how to love myself and really seeing my self-worth. As I looked inward, I gradually found my authenticity and divine truth.

Through the years I experienced a few more heartbreaks with relationships with men. When I made the decision to leave my husband, I was a part of a very strict religion. In this religion divorces are frowned upon. If you decide to divorce, the only grounds allowed are adultery. However, if you chose divorce without adultery, you are not allowed to re-marry. Since there was no cheating in my marriage, I was not free to date, marry, or be intimate with anyone. Premarital sex was not allowed either. The only way I could be free was either committing adultery myself or waiting for my husband to be the guilty one. If either of us did, we would be punished for at least a year. They would announce to the congregation that the person had committed a sin and would be shunned; what they called "disfellowship." We would not be able to talk to anyone in the religion. If we wanted to be accepted back into the church, we would have to attend church faithfully for a year. In the meantime we would have to sit at the back of the church and not interact with anyone. As soon as the meeting was over, you would have to leave. I was not about to put myself through this humiliation. However, I did fall in love deeply with a man from the church. We had to hide this love in fear of judgment and condemnation. Even though we never had a sexual relationship, we did have a very deep emotional attachment. We met in secret and kissed, but never had the courage to take it any further. Eventually the guilt was eating us alive and we ended the love affair. This relationship was one of the most painful endings in my life. This man was my best friend. He gave me love and support when everyone else judged me. Losing him meant I would have to face the church, judgments, and life, all alone. Three years after we ended our forbidden relationship he got engaged. I was devastated because I was still in love with him. Deep down I knew he was marrying someone else to forget me and move on with his life. I remember journaling about the outcome of all of this to later discover everything I had sensed would happen did. A year later I met someone else in the church. He became a very dear friend who was there for me in a time when I suffered a debilitating illness. I loved him dearly and he loved me too. This was six years after my separation but I still wasn't free to be with anyone. We remained friends even though we couldn't formally date, but we had romantic feelings for each other. Eventually we had no choice but to walk away from each other's life since we had no future together. Again, I was heartbroken. This relationship opened my eyes to the insanity of how I was living. I began to see that this was not what God wanted for me and what I wanted for myself. He wanted me to be happy, loved, and supported. He wanted me to have the love of a partner. I began to realize what I was doing to myself and after twenty-one years of being in the religion, I decided it was time to free myself from my self-created prison. Clearly I was brainwashed to value beliefs that kept me from living my authentic self and my divine truth. It was a sigh of relief when I left that religion and freed myself from the prison in my soul.

After losing him, I kept attracting men that weren't emotionally available and wouldn't commit to me. I had to come to the harsh realization that I was attracting these men because I was afraid to commit. Deep down I was emotionally unavailable, and afraid of getting close to anyone, for fear of being abandoned. I was terrified of the idea of giving my heart and soul to someone to then be rejected. Even though they all loved me very much, they felt I wasn't the one. I found myself giving more than I was receiving. These experiences helped me see where I was in my healing journey. They helped me recognize the inner work I still needed around my father figures. I was able to acknowledge my abandonment and rejection issues, and how I never felt important to men. All this triggered the pain of my biological father leaving and never looking for me. He never committed himself to being my father and didn't feel I was important enough to be in his life.

As I saw these men as my teachers, and as an opportunity to grow, it made it a lot easier to forgive them for the hurt they caused me. I became grateful for what I learned about myself. This inspired me to continue to peel the layers of forgiveness. The more I forgave, the happier I became.

Forgiving everyone for what he or she did to me has led me to many insights, blessings, truths, and a better quality of life.

I have learned through forgiveness…

- To love myself and see my worth.
- Everyone has his or her own love language and unique way of expressing love. It doesn't mean I'm not loved, if it's not expressed my way.
- I can be loved and supported through difficult times.
- I can be appreciated for my gifts and talents.
- What you want is not always what you need.
- To give out of love and not out of seeking acceptance.
- I can be loved the way I deserve and be accepted for who I am.
- To not depend on others to fill up my tank.
- To be strong and self-reliant.
- To go after my dreams no matter what others think.
- I don't need anyone to determine my importance. I need to believe I'm important.
- What matters most is what I believe about myself and not what others believe about me.

So how do you forgive? I will walk you through an exercise that will help you forgive others and yourself.

FORGIVING OTHERS

List all the people who have hurt you.

_____

_____

_____

_____

_____

Next to each person, list all the hurtful things that person said or did to you.

_____

_____

_____

_____

_____

Next to the hurtful experience, write the emotion that you were feeling at the time (i.e. anger, sadness, resentment, frustration, pain, etc.)

_____

_____

_____

_____

_____

For each person write down what painful experience he or she had gone through in the past or during his or her life. What wounds did they possibly need to heal?

_____

_____

_____

_____

_____

Go back to your list and identify the emotion you were experiencing and see the connection to what you were feeling verses what they were feeling. If you were feeling anger, most likely they were angry at something or someone. If you were experiencing abuse, most likely they did too. If you felt abandoned, they were probably abandoned by their parents. If you felt neglected or alone, they must have experienced that as well. If you experienced lack of love on their part, they must not have been loved either.

Allow yourself to feel compassion and understanding for their pain as it's the same as your pain. They are human beings doing the best they can with what they have and know. Hurt people hurt others because they don't know how to navigate through their pain. When you allow yourself to feel empathy and compassion for them, you then allow yourself the freedom to heal the hurt they caused you. See them as children of God who deserves love no matter who they are or what wrongs they have done and as worthy of forgiveness for their imperfections and mistakes. Like you they hurt, but don't know how to release their pain without hurting others. Sometimes they are not even aware they are hurting others because they are consumed in their own experience and pain.

Now take a moment and think of the lessons you learned from these experiences. See your responsibility in the hurt that was caused to you. We attract people and situations for our souls to heal. Ask yourself, "How and why did I attract this painful experience to myself?" This is a very import part in your healing, since you will continue to attract the same situation over and over until the lesson has been learned and the healing has taken place. Every painful experience is here to bring to the surface a wound that needs your love and attention. Some wounds take several layers of peeling before healing. What wound in you attracted the painful experience? What did you learn about yourself from the experience? How has this experience helped you become a better person?

_____

_____

_____

_____

_____

These lessons learned become the gift from the wound. These painful experiences are crucial for our soul's evolution. When you can understand the reason you attracted the painful experience and see the lesson, you will find the true blessing. This insight and new view of the situation will automatically create forgiveness in your heart. It will allow you to let go and find peace not only with the person who hurt you but with yourself. As you continue to see that nothing and no one is really here to hurt you, but to help you, then you'll be able to feel gratitude for the painful experience. You will feel gratitude towards those who have hurt you as they were merely helping heal the parts of you that you couldn't recognize.

Now that you are ready to forgive and let go say the following affirmation:

"At this moment I choose to forgive _____ for the pain (he/she) has caused me. I am healed and whole. I choose peace, love, and joy. All that is good surrounds me. I am love."

Finalize it with the following visualization. Review the written version first before listening to the audio at https://soundcloud.com/user-668573947/forgiving-others.

Close your eyes and see the person you need to forgive standing in front of you. Tell him/her everything he/she did that caused you pain. Listen to this person tell you everything you need to hear from him/her to feel peace in your heart. Tell him/her you forgive him/her, and release him/her. Embrace each other, wish each other well, and allow your heart to feel love for him/her. As you're holding each other surround yourself with a white light. For extra love surround each other with a pink light of love.

IMPORTANT: "We release a lot of pain and stress through our tears. Releasing these tears is important throughout your healing process. It's very cleansing to the soul to cry and the quickest way to release pain. You will notice an instant relief after releasing those tears."

FORGIVING YOURSELF

List all the people you have hurt and how you have hurt yourself.

_____

_____

_____

_____

_____

Describe the hurtful things you did to each person and to yourself.

_____

_____

_____

_____

_____

List the wounds you are carrying now and the wounds from the past.

_____

_____

_____

_____

_____

In what ways can you see yourself with compassion?

_____

_____

_____

_____

What positive actions have you done for yourself or others? What qualities do you love about yourself? If you can't think of any, see yourself as a child of God who deserves love no matter who you are or what wrongs you have done, and as worthy of forgiveness for your imperfections and mistakes. See yourself as a human being who is hurting and doesn't know how to channel that pain. You were and are doing the best you can.

Take a moment and think of the lesson to be learned from this experience. See your responsibility in the hurt you have caused yourself or others. Ask yourself, "Why did I hurt someone else? Why did I hurt myself? Where is this coming from?"

_____

_____

_____

_____

_____

Now that you are ready to forgive and let go say the following affirmation:

> *"At this moment I choose to forgive myself for the pain I have caused. I choose to see myself as an imperfect being doing the best I can with what I know. I am healed and whole. I choose peace, love, and joy. All that is good surrounds me. I am love."*

Finalize it with the following visualization. Review the written version first before listening to the audio at https://soundcloud.com/user-668573947/forgiving-yourself.

> *Close your eyes and see the person from whom you need forgiveness standing in front of you. Ask him/her to tell you all that you did to hurt him/her. Tell him/her how sorry you are and ask for forgiveness. Listen to him/her tell you everything you need to hear to feel peace in your heart. After he/she has forgiven you, embrace each other, wish each other well, and allow your heart to feel love for this person. Visualize yourself and the person you have hurt surrounded by a white light. For extra love surround each other with a pink light of love.*

Key 3

Blessing in the Lesson

OUR VIEW OF our painful experiences can either hinder us or bless us. How we choose to see the situation determines how we'll feel. If we choose to focus on the pain and suffering we'll remain in our pain and suffering. However, if we choose to see the blessing in the pain, we'll be able to release the pain and experience inner peace. When we are in a place of suffering we resist the painful experience we are living. However, if we can feel gratitude for the pain, and see it as an opportunity to send love to our wounds, we can then let go of the suffering. Our wounds are craving to be acknowledged and fed love and attention. Even though I understand the behavior of those who have hurt me and I have compassion towards them, it doesn't take away their hurtful behavior. The only way now to heal the hurt is through love. Becoming aware of the parts of the wound that are left to heal, you can now give each part of the wound the love it's been seeking all along. It's important to feel gratitude for the pain and discover what the pain came to teach. Your pain is trying to communicate to you. Listen to what it has to tell you and you will be amazed at what you are holding inside. Each painful experience is for the evolution of our soul. It's in the pain that we grow the most.

In your forgiveness work you were able to identify the lessons learned by the events that caused you pain. In seeing these lessons, you can then open yourself up to see how these experiences are necessary for your growth. Without them we stay stuck; we don't move forward and become the souls we were meant to be.

Relationships are here to mirror us and teach us what we need to work on to become our best. They refine us and show us the areas in ourselves that we have trouble seeing. If we attract a partner who is abusive, this shows us that we lack self-love and self-worth. If we attract people who don't make us a priority, it's because we don't feel important. If we're not being respected, it's because we don't respect ourselves. If we're constantly giving and not receiving, it's because we don't feel deserving. All my past relationships had the same pattern; even though they were different men they all had the same issues. These men didn't have healthy self-esteem and weren't capable of loving themselves or committing to others. I found myself constantly attracting men who were emotionally unavailable and unable to commit to me. As I recognized this pattern I was able to see how emotionally unavailable I was. I wasn't practicing self-love and didn't feel good enough. This discovery has helped me transform those parts of myself.

There is a true blessing in being able to see these aspects of ourselves: it gives us the opportunity to change them. Every relationship I've had has helped me grow and evolve into who I am today. I'm grateful for the pain that led me to the unveiling of my authentic self. If we can focus on what we have learned and work towards improving ourselves, then we will feel blessed for the painful experiences.

"If you want to attract the right person into your life, you must first become what you seek."

When I first attracted my ex-husband, I wasn't aware of my lack of self-worth and self-love. I was sixteen years old and had no clue as to what that even meant. At the time I was living on my own. I couldn't stand my stepfather's abuse anymore and left home. I dropped out of high school and worked a full-time job in a law firm. I dated him for three years before marrying him. I fell in love and believed he would rescue me. I had the false idea that he would make me happy and fulfill all my needs.

We both had suffered traumatic childhoods. We came to one another wounded, seeking acceptance, healing, and unconditional love. A few years into the marriage I became pregnant with my first child. It was one of the most difficult times of my life. Even though I was happy to become a mother, my ex- husband wasn't ready to be a father. He became distant, deprived me of my pregnancy cravings, and was not kind to me. I was very sick through the entire pregnancy and extremely sad. I had nausea, constant dizzy spells, and daily vomiting episodes. This was not what I had imagined being pregnant with my first child would be. This was supposed to be a joyful moment in my life. There began the major challenges in the marriage. The next eight years came with ups, and downs. My body didn't respond well to any types of hormones, and all the birth control attempts made me ill. All of this unsuccessful experimenting led to my second pregnancy. Despite all of my attempts of giving it my all, it's not surprising that eventually the marriage ended. I suggested trying to save our relationship with counseling, aware that we needed to heal our traumas if we wanted our marriage to work. I was willing, but he denied the help. I could have sat there and beaten myself up for marrying the wrong man at such a young age, yet I chose to find the blessing in my experience. I have two amazing sons who inspire me to be the best version of myself. Having my sons led me to create a happy and healthy life for them, and myself.

In this relationship I also discovered the unresolved issues in my soul. I identified where my self-love and self-worth issues had originated. Awareness of my abandonment issues, my relationship with money and my childhood trauma, led to the inner work that helped heal my inner child. The emotional and mental abuse of my marriage was an awakening to my divine truth. I realized one of the most important lessons of my life. I learned no one would truly love me unconditionally until I loved myself unconditionally. Also, I learned I had to see my worth if I wanted others to see it too. And truly the most important lesson of all; no one can make me happy, but ME.

> *"The best relationship you can have is the one you have with yourself. If you want to be loved and respected, you must first love and respect yourself."*

The death of a loved one, especially if unexpected, or the ending of a young life can leave you in deep despair. This loss creates feelings of anger, guilt, denial, confusion, anguish, and a void that's challenging to fill. We wonder how we can see the blessing in such a loss. I know first-hand this devastating feeling. When my twenty-nine-year-old cousin tragically passed away, my world came to a complete halt. At the time life was great. I was living the life I really wanted. I was very excited about what lay ahead. I had just returned from a family trip where we celebrated Christmas and New Year's. Even though things were going well, I remember having a really strange feeling. A few days after the trip, I received a phone call from my mother. She immediately told me my cousin had died. His father found him dead in the bathroom in his house. I couldn't believe what I was hearing. I dropped to the floor and cried for hours. I was inconsolable. My friends came over to try to calm me down and after hours of feeling excruciating pain, I finally was able to fall asleep. The next day I rented a van and picked up other family members and drove out of state for the funeral. I remember getting to my uncle's house where it all happened and feeling my heart sink. As soon as we walked through the door my entire family began to hold each other and cry. The pain was unbearable for us all. When I walked into the bathroom where he was found, I completely lost it. I saw a vision of how this tragedy had happened and my family had to medicate me to calm me down.

My aunt and I were chosen to read the eulogy. I told my uncle I wasn't going to be able to. I was in too much pain and I didn't think I could stop the tears and speak. But my uncle made it clear that my deceased cousin would want me to be the one to read. I arrived at the church and walked up to the coffin and there he was. He looked peaceful and handsome. It was surreal to me that he wasn't alive and breathing. I rubbed his head and it felt the same as when he was alive. He used to shave his hair close to his scalp and it felt fuzzy. I kept rubbing it because it helped me feel as though he was still here. My uncle (his father) completely lost it. He threw himself over the coffin and screamed for his son to wake up. It was one of the most devastating moments to witness the pain of a father lose his child. His other son and I managed to pull him away and sit him on the couch. We held him through his pain.

When it was time for the ceremony to begin, I was very nervous because I didn't think I could do it. As I walked up towards the podium I felt a calm come over me. I was able to stop the tears and speak. I truly believe my cousin was right beside me the entire time. Soon after the hearse took my cousin away. In that moment I knew I would never

see him again until I took my last breath. I ran after the hearse scream-
ing in agony to please bring him back. My son had to grab me and
calm me down. This was a pain I had never felt in my entire life. I felt
like a big part of me was ripped from my soul. In that moment I lost
complete touch with who I really was. Soon after we went back to my
uncle's home where we gathered to begin mourning our loss. The pain
was overwhelming and I had to be medicated to get through the grief.
The dose they gave me was very high and all I did was sleep-- the only
way I felt some relief from the agony. When we arrived back home all I
could do was cry. For three weeks I lay in bed and just cried. My cousin's
spirit came to me several times. He showed up with his mother and told
me how happy he was being with her. He had missed her terribly and
wanted to be with her desperately his entire life on earth. He had finally
recieved his wish. He kept telling me to get up, but I just couldn't.
Finally after three weeks of grieving, I got up and went on with my life
as best as I could.

I couldn't shake off the guilt I was carrying. All these questions and
what ifs began to surface. I blamed myself for not being there enough.
I blamed myself for not convincing him to move in with me. I blamed
myself for not being able to help him. The guilt was heavy on my soul.
Even though everyone told me it wasn't my fault or anyone's fault, I
couldn't stop believing that it was. I knew I had to let go of the guilt
and release him. His soul needed to rest in peace and I didn't want to
keep him attached to my earthly suffering. I knew he wanted to see me
happy and not grieve him more than necessary.

If it wasn't for all the healing tools I had at the moment, I would
have not been able to get through this deeply painful loss. Through
time and a lot of inner work on my part, I was able to mourn, grieve his
loss, and reach acceptance to a certain degree. But I did struggle for a

long time to let him go. It truly has been a journey letting him go even though I know he's in a wonderful place surrounded by love and family.

I began to focus on the happy moments we had shared. He was very funny and brought a lot of joy to others. He had jokes for everything. His charming personality made him extremely loveable and women adored him. He was amazing with his nieces and nephews. He loved children even though he never had his own. I know he would have made a great father. There were times he lived with me and that was not always easy. He had a challenging temper and could be hard headed at times. We used to have these intense arguments. He would come to me for advice and would get very angry when I would tell him truths he didn't want to hear. But we always made up afterwards. The love was greater than the disagreement. When he lost his mother at the age of eleven, I tried my best to always be there for him. I still have all the letters he wrote me sharing the gratitude for everything I did for him. Somehow it always felt that I never did enough.

We always shared very spiritual and deep conversations. He loved spirituality and he loved helping others. He was truly gifted in many ways and made a difference to every life he encountered. He was loved greatly for the amazing soul he was on earth and is now in heaven. He had a heart of gold. I was blessed to have him in my life as long as I did. I chose to remember the happy memories I shared with him which brought me solace. I remembered the good times, smiles, laughter, and joy he brought to my life. However, before I was able to remember the good, I allowed myself the time to lie in bed and cry it out for weeks. I didn't rush the process. I understood I had to feel the pain in order to heal. Once I gave myself permission to mourn and grieve him, then I was able to focus on the memory of my cousin.

My cousin's life had been taking a turn in a bad direction. If he had continued to live, he would have had a difficult life. When I think of him finding peace and being with his deceased loved ones in heaven, I find solace. He had a terribly difficult time overcoming the loss of his mother. He struggled with depression most of his life. I now know he's with her in heaven. My deep love for him only wants what's best for him. I believe this peace is what his spirit needed. I remember knowing his death would lead to major changes that were needed in our family. His death had a lot of purpose as it motivated some family members to follow their dreams--including me. His passing brought all my fears to the surface for healing and triggered all the unhealed trauma my son had not realized. It has led and inspired us both to seek healing and face our fears. I would not have had the deep self-reflection if my cousin had not passed away. He had repeated that my gifts were needed in the world and I needed to share them. He inspires me to continue my life's work in helping humanity. After his passing I began to feel the calling to create a healing center to help people with addiction and those who are labeled with some type of disorder. Many people with these issues haven't been able to live successful lives because they are missing the help they need. I believe when you combine the holistic, spiritual, and medical in recovery, massive change occurs. I have experienced it myself and with those I have helped. This healing center will be open to anyone in need. No one will be turned away. The work in this center will be in his honor. I don't know when or how this will come about, but I will not stop until this center is alive and running.

Both of his talented brothers, who are music artists, have become even more passionate. I see their determination to live their dreams of making it big. You can see how their music has evolved as well as the passion behind their lyrics. I know their brother's passing has a lot to do with their success. I know he's a driving force in their lives.

What's even more amazing to me is watching his father continue to live. He hasn't let the passing of his son stop him from living. His other children inspire him to keep going. He continues to work, spend time with friends, enjoy his grandchildren, and be there for his other children. This pain could have easily made him give up on life, but it didn't. The grief only made him stronger and an inspiration to those who watch him continue to live with his loss. It doesn't mean he doesn't miss his son every day or not feel the void; he just chooses not to let this heartache stop him from living. He sees his son as an angel in heaven who is happy and helping the family here on earth. That brings him some level of peace.

Some deaths we will never understand, but trust we all choose a divine time to be born and to leave our bodies. Our bodies may no longer be here, but our souls are eternal. I tend to not use the word "death" and prefer to say a soul has passed. I once heard the analogy that we unzip our bodies and return to our true selves. We are spirit beings in a human body. Our souls never die. All the loved ones who have crossed over are still with us. They never truly ever leave us. Find ways to keep yourself connected to them as they are waiting for you to ask them for help. It brings them great joy to help you in any way they can.

If we can see the blessing in having shared wonderful moments with our loved ones who have passed and not focus on losing them, then we can find the blessing in the pain. Understand that overcoming our grief takes time; it's a process. Be patient with yourself and use these tools to help ease the grief. Keep in mind it's not time that heals; it's what you do in that time that creates the healing. Everyone heals at his or her own pace and in his or her own way, but find healthy ways to work through the process, and most important have faith that your pain will subside. You definitely need to allow yourself a time period to mourn and grieve, but don't prolong it more than necessary. Be kind and loving towards yourself during this healing process. Forgive yourself for any guilt you may carry, and most of all be patient with yourself by not rushing the process. Seek outside help whether it be with a grief counselor or a spiritual healer. Grief is not something to go through on your own. Getting help will alleviate the suffering and will give you the tools you need to process the pain in a healthy way.

Another area that can create suffering is our careers. Sometimes we are faced with bosses and co-workers we don't get along with or have jobs we don't enjoy. Waking up every day and feeling like we're dragging ourselves to a place we don't want to be can be quite difficult. However, there is a reason we are drawn to these jobs and the people in them. If we have a boss who's unfair and constantly treating employees with disrespect, understand we attracted him or her because we're not loving and respecting ourselves. If we are surrounded by deceitful people who lie and cheat to get ahead, there is a part of us that is not being honest with ourselves. When we love, respect, and are living in authenticity, there is no way we will put up with a negative job situation for a very long time. Sometimes there are qualities in ourselves that need to be refined. If we are not patient, or get easily frustrated, we are learning to improve those parts of ourselves. Difficult bosses and co-workers are teacher's too. Once we can identify why we're attracting these harmful patterns we'll have the power to change them. We'll know what we need to shift in us in order to create the work environment we seek. This awareness will not only lead us to self- improvement, but to becoming a better employee. It will also help us identify what is our ideal career and drive us to go after what we *really* want. That will be the blessing in the lesson.

Before I discovered what my life's mission was, I had to go through many work experiences. Each one was leading me to grow in ways that guided me to where I am today. I began working with top leaders at a very young age. Throughout my life I had gained experience working with authors promoting their books, and they supplied insight when I was ready to promote my own book. Helping executives with their travel arrangements taught me the best ways to travel for my own events. Overseeing and supporting sales teams, helped me learn what it takes to sell myself, and during the process I realized it's not my gift or calling. Budgeting for top accounts has been a great tool for my own personal and business finances. Writing promotional material, proposals, emails and letters for CEOs and VPs has given me insights as I build a coaching career. Communicating with co-workers, clients, customers, and leaders taught me how to relate to different personalities with sincere vulnerability. I now have deep compassion and understanding for the people I help. Dealing with difficult people, not only customers, but also in the work place, led me to discover the healing power of meditation. I also found programs, spiritual teachers, workshops, love mentors, and business coaches, who led me to my position today. All these work experiences were necessary to realize my life's mission.

The same applies to our relationship with money. If we find ourselves constantly broke or always struggling to pay our bills it can be very frustrating, especially if we can't give to our loved ones. The good news is, as with everything else, we have the power to change, and believe it or not there is a blessing behind it all. If we're struggling financially this is an indicator of a false belief and wound we have around money. The same way we create relationships with people, we do with money. Our parents or caretakers play a huge role in our view of money. We pick up their bad habits and false belief system regarding money as early as infancy. Their relationship with money becomes ours. If you can go back and identify their relationship with money, you'll be able to see your own. This knowledge will lead you to an awareness that has kept money from you. The moment you can change that pattern and false belief system, you'll be able to change your experience with money, which will lead to a healthy view of money, which will in turn attract the money you seek.

Before I knew that a relationship with money existed, I was struggling to make ends meet. There were a few occasions when I had to resort to government help. Even though I always worked, I couldn't seem to make enough. At the time I wasn't aware of the help that was available concerning money issues. One thing I did know, what was impossible for me, was not impossible for God. I began praying about my finances and built my faith around attracting more money. I started to believe that money was coming to me. I believed God was taking care of me and making sure all my needs were met. This worked beautifully. I didn't realize at the time I was applying the law of attraction. I started to attract more money than ever before. I no longer struggled to pay my bills. I even had money to take my sons on vacation and do fun family activities. Sometimes I even had money in savings. I was content living this way. It felt really good having peace regarding money. However, I noticed all my friends made a lot more money than me. They were able to have a lot more freedom. I became curious as to why I was not attracting money at that level. A few years later I was blessed to come across a program that helped me identify my relationship with money. I realized my relationship with money stemmed from my parent's relationship with money. My stepfather made a lot of money, but it was either drug-related or through scams. His money was dirty and he never enjoyed it. We still lived as if we were poor. He would stash it away in the bank. My mother on the other hand gave all her money away. Here I am, believing money is dirty and I should give it all away. To make matters worse I also was relating money to my biological father. He was never there for me and I thought of money in the same way. These discoveries helped me shift my financial beliefs, resulting in attracting more monetary abundance. Most essential are the peace and ease that accompanied changing my relationship with money. Now I have more than enough and I attract money with greater ease.

We live in a world where many suffer from illnesses. There is this false conception of how illnesses are created. Many people believe it's all genetics and they have no control over their illnesses. However, illnesses truly stem from our emotions, and our mental programming. Some are even related to past life experiences. I know this first hand. When I was in my late twenties my body completely shut down. I couldn't stand, walk, shower or even feed myself. I was completely immobile and in severe pain. Even the hairs on my body hurt. I was tested for several diseases and cancer became a real possibility. This was a scary time in my life. I was a single mother of two small children and I was working in a place I really loved. I was happy helping authors promote their books and loved my job and I knew I would lose my job if I didn't recover quickly.

After several tests I was diagnosed with Fibromyalgia Syndrome, which affects the nervous system, muscles and soft tissue. The symptoms include chronic pain in the muscles, fatigue, sleep problems and painful tender points or trigger points at certain parts of the body. The doctor informed me that it's not curable. I would live with this disease for the rest of my life. He suggested I apply for disability and move to a warmer climate. I went home feeling devastated. I wondered what my life would become and what I couldn't give my children. I couldn't stand the idea of my children growing up with a sick mother and a life of poverty. I had always wanted more for my children and myself.

Here I was lying in bed, in pain, with the uncertainty of my future. However, I was blessed to have the incredible support of friends and family. Not only did they take care of me, they also were proactive in caring for my children. As I lay in bed in pain for hours, many questions surfaced. Through the pain and the tears, and journaling, I discovered how I had created this illness. Even though I had been through traditional therapy, it had only landed me this far. I realized this pain was unhealed trauma of my childhood, and painful marriage, stored in my body. This experience forced me to look within. I wanted to heal my body, but I knew I first needed to heal my mind and soul. Even though I lost my job I gained much more than I could have ever imagined. Being sick was leading me to changing my entire life. I was determined to prove the doctors wrong. I knew I had the power to heal myself. I was determined to be healthy for my children and provide them with a life of excellence.

I began my inner journey reading self-improvement books, most of them provided me with healing tools. Also, I found several healing modalities that were more effective than traditional therapy. Through journaling I realized I needed to change my life in a drastic way. I decided to move to a place where I could have a slower-paced life. This was an opportunity to let go of the past and start anew. This move gave me the opportunity to walk away from a religion that had me prisoner in my mind and heart. It was holding me back from living my divine truth and living in authenticity. I began seeking out spiritual teachers and healers. As I worked on healing my trauma, my body healed along with my soul. I beat the odds, proving the doctors wrong. This painful experience was a rebirth. I transformed in ways I never would have, if I hadn't become sick in the first place. Through my illness I found my inner peace and learned ways to ground myself. I moved to the place of my dreams and found my mission on earth. What's interesting is how this experience would be an example for my older son later on in his life.

"Transformation is not meant to be easy. It's the death of the old self and the birth of the renewed soul. It requires the courage to go deep into your pain and recognize the source. In the process one must be willing to navigate through the anguish, fear, and programming that was created. As you heal each layer of pain, you will begin to experience the calming of the burdened soul."

When my son was a child, I knew he was different. I sensed he wasn't like everyone else. He was quite challenging and at times I had no clue how to deal with him. I was a very young mother and never really had anyone to teach me how to be a mother. I had to figure all this out on my own. I'm sure I made a lot of mistakes as I tried to navigate through motherhood. It's difficult enough with a child who displays what society calls "normal behavior," but when your child doesn't behave like other children, it can be quite challenging. I took him to several doctors and they all said he would outgrow the behavior. I searched for books and anything that would guide me. I even took parenting classes, but nothing helped. One day I received a magazine from my church and on the cover there was a young child with a frustrated look on his face. He was trying to complete his homework but was struggling. On the cover was the question: *Is your child suffering from ADD (Attention Deficit Disorder)?* As I read through the magazine, everything described mimicked my son's behavior. At the time he was only three years old and there was nothing the doctors could do until he started school. Even though he was not formally diagnosed, it was still a big relief knowing what I was dealing with. I began to research ADD and how to parent this kind of child which was really helpful. I saw an improvement in his behavior as I changed mine. When he started kindergarten I requested an evaluation. I wanted to make sure my son was going to receive everything he needed to succeed. I wasn't surprised when they diagnosed him with ADHD (Attention Deficit Hyperactivity Disorder) and OCD (Obsessive Compulsive Disorder). At the time I wasn't very familiar with disorders and medications. This was all new to me. I was against putting him on any medication and chose the holistic route. I believed he could succeed with other types of help, but I remained open to medication in case the other resources didn't work. The holistic route seemed to work beautifully for him. We also implemented a daily routine and made sure he was kept mentally and physically stimulated with activities, occupational therapy, and speech therapy. I made sure he avoided certain foods and used guided meditations, prayer, and spirituality to help him mentally and emotionally. Most important, I was able to recognize that his behavior was a reflection of my own. If I were upset, frustrated, angry, or agitated he would misbehave. I sought ways to keep calm as I knew my well-being affected his. I took responsibility for how I was affecting my child and did everything in my power to be the best mother and person he needed.

When I entered the mental health world I saw a lot of things I didn't agree with. Personally I have a hard time with labels and medicating everyone. I believe this creates a false identity of self and keeps people stuck in a world of limitations. Many are gifted and talented souls who are simply wired differently. They just need to learn how to manage their gifts.

I was never formally diagnosed with any disorders, because that wasn't very common in my generation. Knowing what I know now, I would have easily been labeled with ADD and Schizophrenia. I realize medication was not my personal journey. The holistic approach worked best for me. When I suffered moments of deep depression, the doctors tried several medications, but for some reason they just didn't work for me. I know there are people who benefit greatly from medication, but it made me sick to my stomach to witness many doctors overmedicating to the point of disabling people. I didn't want to become someone going through life like a zombie and I chose to go the holistic route. The journey I chose helped me discover a deep understanding for my son and myself. This awareness helped me use the right approach in helping my son. Through his journey I learned a lot about my own. I also learned a lot about what the world calls disorders. There is a lot more to it than the mental health world understands about people like my son and me. We are wired differently for a reason. Most people who are labeled with a disorder have a gift and when managed can be a great blessing to the world. The healers, teachers, artists, musicians, actors, inventors, and those meant to bring change to the world are usually labeled with some kind of disorder. Some of us need medication to manage the gift and some of us don't. If we carry unhealed trauma, it activates the imbalanced part of our gift which leads to negative reactions and behaviors that can consume our lives. For some the medication can be a great benefit as they navigate through the pain and learn how to manage their mind and emotions. Eventually some can wean off the medications and thrive while others can't. I have discovered the more gifted the person is the more he or she will need medication. Their gift can overpower them to the point of not being able to function. In those cases I support medication. Everyone is unique and has a different journey. It all depends on what the person signed up to experience on his or her divine contract.

When I was raising my son, I didn't see things this clearly yet. Throughout his life he was told how his life would be limited and all that he would have to endure. Doctors are very helpful in many ways; however they don't determine the outcome of our lives. I taught my son this principle since childhood. The only one who truly knows our destiny is God. He listened to my guidance and ignored all the naysayers and went off to achieve success. He was always on the honor roll, won many awards even one from the President of the United States. Through the years he continued to be the best at everything he chose to accomplish.

At the age of fifteen he suffered a football injury that left him physically disabled. He dislocated his hip and the emergency room doctor didn't catch it in time. This created severe sciatic nerve damage and he had no feeling in his leg and foot. The doctors said he would never walk the same again. He would have to wear a brace for the rest of his life and wouldn't be able to play sports again. He was devastated! He underwent two surgeries and a year of rehabilitation. Even though the doctor's report didn't look good, I believed in the healing power of God. I knew he could heal my son and restore him better than he was before. He was using a wheel chair, crutches, and a brace to get around. He couldn't attend school and had a special teacher helping him at home. He missed out on his freshman year of high school and his friends walked away. Through it all I kept telling him not to give up. I encouraged him not to listen to the doctors and to have faith that he could heal. In the middle of all this we were also dealing with a malpractice lawsuit against the emergency room doctor. I felt a lot of turmoil, pain, and uncertainty. Through this pain I didn't lose my faith. I kept breathing hope into his heart. Eventually his injury healed. He still didn't have full feeling in his toes, but he no longer needed a wheelchair, crutches, and even the brace. He was able to walk, run, and even play sports. Again beating the odds!

After he recovered from the injury, he started to suffer from depression. He was left with trauma from the accident. He was struggling accepting what happened. He had never experienced anything tragic before and it was difficult for him to accept his reality. Missing out on high school, friends, sports, and the normal things teenagers do in life, took its toll on him. For the following two years he struggled with find-ing acceptance and peace. His depression consumed him and he was placed in a special school. He couldn't handle the normal demands of a regular high school. He began to feel like a failure. He became suicidal and I couldn't leave him home alone. He was put on anti-depressants and mood-stabilizer. He was now facing a new label: Bipolar. I was blessed at the time to be working for an understanding boss who let me work from home. I was committed to helping my son heal and overcome his darkness. His father and I hired a tutor and he was able to catch up with school. He ended his junior year on the honor roll and won an award for the Kid of Character in our county. He was starting to find hope for his future and believe in himself. That year we won the lawsuit and decided to take a family trip for the holidays to New York. I had just reconciled with my biological father and was going to meet with fam-ily. We had a wonderful time and returned feeling joy and were looking forward to a bright future. A few days after we returned from our trip, we received the devastating news that my twenty-nine-year-old cousin had tragically died. I was very surprised at how well my son handled the news. We packed up a rental van, picked up family members along the way, and headed towards the funeral.

When we returned he received another blow. Since he wasn't able to physically attend his freshman year in high school, he didn't have enough credits to graduate. This was the icing on the cake, another major challenge in his life to face when he still had not recovered from the previous ones. Months later I had a coaching event in a town a few hours from where we lived. My son was going to come with me to help me set up my booth and monitor it while I was coaching. I noticed he was a little off during our drive. He wasn't himself but I didn't think much of it. When we arrived at the hotel a very strange feeling came over us both. We walked in to the hotel room, but something felt off in that room. My son and I immediately felt dark entities roaming the hotel halls. There was a huge cockroach in the bathroom sink that completely threw us off even more. That night we didn't get any sleep. We were both restless. I had no idea how I was going to have the energy to work at the event.

It was early morning when I finally began to fall asleep. Then I heard my son leaving the room. I asked him where he was going and he was on his way to get some continental breakfast. A few minutes later the hotel phone rings. The front clerk said my son was being transported to the hospital. I ran to see what was happening and found a police officer with the front desk clerk. As they were explaining that my son was having a breakdown, I was in complete and utter shock. They escorted him to the hospital and I met him there. I was shocked and confused. It turned out that this trip triggered the death of my cousin and a past life event. He was hospitalized for a week and I had to stay in a hotel until he was released. I ended up checking out of that hotel room and found a much better one with great energy.

After a week of hospitalization he began to feel better and was released. Before all of this happened, he was weaned off the anti-depressants and mood-stabilizers. In the hospital they put him back on mood-stabilizers. When we got back home, he decided not to take the medication and try to live without them.

Two weeks later he decided to sleep over a friend's house. He stayed there longer than he planned. Apparently he was displaying odd behavior and his friend's mother brought him home. She called me when she was on her way to drop him off. After a while, I realized he should have been home. I found it odd and called his friends mother to see what happened. She said she had dropped him off an hour ago. That scared me and I went outside to see if I could find him. He was on the sidewalk looking at the sky. I felt something wasn't right. I knew something was off. I brought him upstairs and for the next few days his behavior was completely bizarre.

On the morning of my birthday, I noticed he was a lot worse. I asked my male friend to come over to help me with him. I didn't know what to do. My friend saw how he was behaving and told me to take him to the hospital. My son didn't want to go and I had to call an ambulance. A police officer came over and my son was locked in the bathroom. I was scared. I didn't understand what was happening. I though the ambulance would come, not a police officer. Soon after several officers showed up. Finally they talked him into going with them peacefully to the hospital. My son was disorientated. It was as if he were not presently there, as if he were traveling to another dimension. I had to watch them handcuff my son and take him away in a police car as if he were some criminal. I was confused and in a lot of pain. He was hospitalized for three weeks. In those three weeks he would call me every day with these messages he was hearing and the things he was seeing. He didn't want to be there, but he knew he had to stay. It wasn't safe for him to be home. Plus at the time I had no idea what was happening and how to handle it. He was put back on his mood-stabilizers. When he came home he needed twenty-four hour care. Thank God I worked from home and was able to be there for him. He was constantly suffering from panic attacks, anxiety, and traveling to different dimensions. He felt he was being attacked by demons and lived in terror every day.

These emotional and mental breakdowns led to several hospitalizations and the unpleasant world of medication exploration. Doctors were confused and started labeling him with several disorders. First they thought he had Attention Deficit Hyperactivity Disorder, next they believed he was Bipolar, and then they considered Schizophrenia. Since they weren't sure they diagnosed him Schizoaffective, which is a combination of Bipolar and Schizophrenia. As he sought out different doctors, they all had different opinions. I knew the doctors and medications could only do so much. I knew he was reacting to unhealed trauma. I believed once he found healing from those traumatic events, he would no longer have the symptoms that looked like multiple disorders. I tried showing him healthier ways to heal, but he wasn't ready for my help. He had to find out the truth his way. After a year of trying different medications, and several hospitalizations, his mental health continued to deteriorate. I found the medications created new symptoms, and I was beside myself with grief and frustration. I had suffered through many things in life, but nothing topped seeing my son sick, in agony, and pleading to die. There were times I prayed to God to save my son from his agony. I even asked God to relieve his pain and take him. I was willing to live a life of pain without him in return for his suffering to end. I never experienced pain at this deep level. I thought I knew pain when my cousin died until I was helpless seeing my child in agony.

Finally the doctors decided the best thing for him would be long-term treatment. They suggested a hospital that provided everything he would need to get better. I endured seven months of my son's hospitalization. Instead of sending him off to college, I had to face the reality of my son in a psychiatric hospital. The place turned out to be nothing like the doctors described. It was a very scary and violent place. Patients were getting beaten, raped and abused. He experienced things I never imagined a child of mine would ever have to endure. But the experience in that place showed him his inner strength, resilience, and God's power. He learned he had the power to control his emotions. He discovered that medication wasn't the only answer. Even though he did need the medicine, he still needed to heal the pain that was causing his breakdown. All this time he had been trying desperately to numb the pain and not face the pain. He built his faith up and his relationship with God. Most important, he saw God's power over his life. He began to look inside himself and heal the wounds of the past that were keeping him stuck in the present. He was finally ready for my help. I began using Integrated Energy Therapy and the Akashic Records to help him heal. Slowly I began to see his soul emerge from the pain and start to experience relief through healing. The doctor was able to lower his medication significantly and send him home.

My son left that place without a scratch. While everyone around him was experiencing violence, God kept him safe from harm. He learned things there that he never would have learned in any college. No degree would compensate for the valuable lessons he gained, which will carry him through his entire life. What a blessing in disguise!

After he was out of the hospital I was sure the worst was over, but to my surprise we were not out of the woods yet. I ended up losing my financial stability and had to relocate to another state. This was quite devastating for us all. We had to let go of the life we knew and create a new one. We experienced poverty to the level of being on government assistance. I went from living in a three-bedroom house, to sharing a room with my sons, and sleeping on mattresses on the floor. Everything that I had built was completely gone. I couldn't understand why this was all happening, but I knew there was a divine reason, and I trusted God's plan.

A year and a half later my son and I made the decision to try to see how he would do off medication. He was coping really well emotionally and mentally, but kept feeling something was holding him back. He had no motivation to get out into the world and live. We thought the reasons could possibly be the medication. Even though he was on a very low dose, we believed it wouldn't make that much of a difference if he got off the drug. We were both excited and nervous as we had no idea what to expect. However, we were positive and expected a great outcome. I consulted my angels and received guidance in helping wean him off the meds. He seemed to be doing really well. We even celebrated how well he was doing medication-free. Then two weeks later he began to experience insomnia. He tried sleeping aids, but nothing was helping him sleep. I wanted to take him to the doctor, but he kept refusing to go. He was determined not to get back on medication. My younger son and I began to see changes in him that were of great concern. He was not sleeping at all for an entire week. I begged him to see the doctor as I sensed what was coming. One night that week, I called my friend in a panic. I was terrified. I felt something bad was about to happen. I was very anxious. I remember her saying: "Your son is about to become independent and that scares you. It's time to let him go." I wasn't sure what that letting go would look like, but I would soon find out.

I went to bed that night still feeling anxious. It was about 1:00 AM when I suddenly woke up. I went into my son's room and he was wide-awake. I knew something wasn't right. He wasn't himself. In that moment I knew I had to take him to the hospital. He was traveling to different dimensions. He was detaching from the 3D world. I remember saying to myself: "This is what doctors call mania." My younger son called 911 and when the paramedics arrived they recognized he was having what doctors call a manic episode, which occurs when someone's Bipolar. He ended up in the hospital for an entire month. He was so out of it that I rarely spoke to him and he didn't want visitors. That was very difficult for me because every time he was hospitalized I talked to him daily. I even saw him several times a week for hours at a time. This hospital only allowed visitors for a period of two hours on the weekend and one day a week. He was going through this on his own. This is when I understood my friend's words-- I had to let him go as he was getting ready to become independent. I had to allow him the space to heal his way and to process without me. He was showing me that he no longer needed me to get through his hospitalizations. He had matured. I was very proud of how he handled the entire experience. It took several months after for him to finally feel normal again. It was shocking and traumatic for us all. I blamed myself for getting him off the medication. I was carrying a lot of pain and guilt over everything that happened. I blamed myself for my son's suffering and setback. I was suffering from anxiety and panic attacks as I couldn't stop beating myself up for what I had done to my son.

Fast-forward almost a year later and we realized getting him off the medication was actually a blessing in disguise. Through this experience he discovered a lot about himself; especially that medication wasn't holding him back. It was actually helping him. He realized that fear of success was the true cause of his lack of motivation. He discovered his true gifts and healing abilities to help those in need. He realized how powerful he truly is. He sees his journey with more clarity and understanding. He no longer suffers from his journey, but is beginning to understand he chose all of this. All of these painful experiences and even being Bipolar that has consumed him and his life. He understands now that his mental imbalance and wiring is really a gifted mind with strong healing abilities. He's slowly working on accepting and loving himself. Without all of these experiences he wouldn't have the awareness, knowledge, and wisdom he has at such a tender age. All of these painful experiences have led us both to healing modalities. It led him to become a Reiki healer and it led me to Akashic Records and Integrated Energy Therapy. We were also guided to Transcendental Meditation.

Now he continues to work on his inner peace daily. He understands himself more and knows how to manage his anxiety and anger. When he's overwhelmed, he will cry, and talk about his feelings instead of allowing his negative emotions get the best of him. He practices meditation, journals and enjoys exercising. Even though he continues to heal, grow, and evolve, and work towards finding his balance, he now knows he has the power to create his story. We may have lived with a story for years, but we can create a new, positive, happy story. He's beginning to understand that how the world sees a disorder is in reality a gifted mind. Had he not experienced all these painful experiences, he never would have learned the incredible lessons that are leading him to his greatness. He now understands he has a big mission in helping humanity.

Through my son's painful journey I realized I chose to be part of the mental health world. I know I'm here to help change how the world views the unique minds and souls of those they label as suffering with disorders. My stepfather, ex-husband, cousin, and son all chose the journey of being Bipolar. Which means I chose it as well. It has been, and still is, a huge part of my journey. I chose it because I want the world to see its beauty. They are merely gifted healers who come to create change in the world. By showing up imbalanced they create balance in others. As people's wounds are triggered through their behavior, and healing occurs, balance is restored in the person. They come with a lot of their own trauma which needs to heal, and this creates the imbalance in their brains, which is a major sacrifice. Even though they seem cold and heartless at times, they really are very sensitive souls who seek love and acceptance. However, as they help others heal…they heal as well. Eventually the imbalance can subside with the right help. They have brilliant minds filled with creativity and ground-breaking ideas. They have the ability to run corporations and create inventions that change how the world works. Their brilliant minds come with endless possibilities. Once they discover how to manage the chemical imbalance, which is triggered by trauma, they can live some of the most successful lives.

The world needs to change how they view them and see the beauty they bring to the world. But we live in a world where ego is dominant and the behavior is seen instead of what's behind the behavior. I hope to change that before I leave this planet. I thank all my loved ones who choose the Bipolar journey as they are my greatest teachers and healers. Helping people who are labeled with a disorder has become my life's passion. I'm determined to help them see their true beauty and the special souls that they are. I want them to feel loved and accepted and honored for their divine gifts--not as damaged people with nothing to offer. I want them not to focus on their label, but instead tap into their gifts and talents and use them to make a difference in the world. This will help them see their worth and no longer feel like rejected outcasts.

Being the mother of this incredible child has showed me my own inner strength, which has led me to many great things. It was clear I had to be an example for him to follow by being positive, practice self-care, and have the unshakable faith that God would work a miracle in him. This inspired me to be at my highest with my self-love and spiritual practices. My faith grew stronger than ever. I found amazing love mentors who helped me discover my life's mission as an author and a speaker. I learned what true abundance is and how to attract it. My relationship with my son blossomed to depths I never could have imagined. My life completely changed for the better. I always said that every tragedy comes with a blessing. In my case it came with many life- changing miracles. At the time my younger son was an amazing support system for his brother. I was blessed with all his accomplishments in school and in his life. He was thriving! When my older son was going through all his hospitalizations, I found the quality time with my younger son very healing. We found a lot of new places to visit together and shared magical times. I focused on the son who was doing great. This helped me be strong for the son who needed all my support. I focused on my blessings and that made a world of difference.

Having lost my financial stability and having to move to a different state to begin a new life at first was quite devastating. I really loved where I lived and enjoyed my lifestyle. I had to let all of that go and live in a place I really didn't like or enjoy. I had to let go of my dreams of being a coach, writer, and speaker, and go back to corporate America when I had left that life years ago. Thankfully my family came through with all the love and support they could possibly provide. They all put their financial resources together and paid for all my expenses as I transitioned.

I went from living in sunny beautiful paradise, working on the beach with my laptop and cell phone, to sitting in a cubicle for eight hours. I didn't even have money to put food on the table and had to resort to government assistance. I couldn't afford a place to live and my family offered their homes. I had several choices, but I chose the state that would have more opportunities for me and my sons.

Living with family was not a pleasant experience. There was a lot of drama amongst them and fighting. They didn't really have room for us and it was very challenging. For a few months we went back and forth from one home to the next. Finally, after several months, I had enough income to at least rent a room. My mother was gracious enough to let me stay in her room which was the biggest in her apartment. I was able to share it with my adult sons. They slept on mattresses on the floor, and I slept on the only bed in the room. I was also able to help her a little financially as she was also struggling. The neighborhood was very dangerous too. Every morning I faced the homeless people sleeping on the cold sidewalks, watched them sick with hunger, and felt the pain of those struggling with addictions and mental health. It was my daily reminder that at least I had a roof over my head, heat to keep us warm, food to calm the hunger, clothes to shelter our bodies, and family who loved us. It was a very humbling experience and a reminder to be grateful of the blessings I had even if they were minimal at the time. To make matters worse, my health began to deteriorate. My body was definitely feeling the shock and stress of the major changes in my life.

As all this was happening I completely forgot about everything I knew and didn't remember who I was. I lost my identity--at least I thought I did. I felt helpless, sad, beaten, negative, afraid, and lost the faith that use to be my driving force. I couldn't understand how all this was happening to me. I was always able to support my sons and myself. How did I get here? Why did I get here? What did I do wrong? These were the questions that were consuming my every being.

Before all this happened I felt I was doing everything right. I was making all my self-care practices a priority to the point of joining a one-year program which focused primarily on self-love. I practiced everything the program taught me to the "T." I was meditating and doing all my positive visualizations. I was using my IET for healing, and was full of faith, believing only blessings and abundance were coming. It didn't make any sense to me everything that happened. I was consumed in the pain and loss that I couldn't see how this was all a piece of the puzzle. Little did I know that this was all part of manifesting my heart's desires.

After seven months things began to turn around. I manifested a job that allowed me to save for a better place to live and soon after I manifested a really nice apartment in one of the best neighborhoods. This was a joyous time for us and slowly my faith began to emerge. I made really special friends who helped me remember who I am and why this all happened. One of the biggest things that helped me was remembering how everything is pre-chosen. I chose this experience.

For a long time I was judging what I was feeling. I felt it was wrong to resist and not accept my journey. I really struggled being back in corporate America. I held on to that resistance for a very long time. I was resisting "resisting." I needed to surrender that it's okay to resist. I was definitely negotiating with life by wanting a different life than I was experiencing. I was completely judging my own journey. I know I chose this life exactly as it is, but yet I continued to reject it instead of honoring it. There was a lot of beauty in that moment in my life, but my resistance wasn't allowing me to see it all.

I also wasn't fully allowing myself to mourn and grieve the life that I felt I had lost. It's almost as though I felt I "shouldn't" because I'm "supposed" to accept that all is perfect. However, I had to allow myself to be human and give myself permission to feel the loss at its fullest in order to release it.

After this awareness I began to send love to the corporate environment and to the resistance. I asked the angels to show me the lessons from this new work experience. They revealed that the lesson was to accept and surrender to where I was being sent to help humanity. To look at it as missionary work. Throughout my entire life I moved around a lot due to circumstances. For years I wished I could live a more stable life, which I had experienced for seven years. But then I realized it was God sending me where I was needed. I was not being sent to third world countries, but I was being sent to environments that were not easy to handle. However, I helped a lot of people in the process. I needed to begin to see the corporate world with those same eyes. This was my missionary work. Missionary work comes with letting go of certain comforts, but it also brings a lot of fulfillment. While I was in the corporate environment I met some amazing people whose lives I helped heal and change. During this time, I also encountered someone who suffered from major mood swings. He was not easy to deal with, but I knew he was here to teach me something. He reminded me of my stepfather who had found fault in everything I did; in his eyes I could not do anything right. He always found ways to point out what he believed I did wrong. He never pointed out the good I accomplished. This was merely an opportunity to heal and to let go of the past and embrace the amazing future God had in store for me. Letting the past go was going to help me build unshakable courage to get out into the world with my message.

Years ago I had fought with my stepfather all the time. Every time he attacked me, I attacked back. Since then I have learned attacking isn't the right way to handle situations. Speaking my truth lovingly and staying true to myself is how I stand in my power without giving it away by feeding into negative behavior. The more I practiced, the more I was able to stay true to myself when the time came to be in the public eye. I knew this was preparing me for what was to come. When you are a powerful speaker there are moments when people will believe you're wrong or will judge your beliefs, wisdom and insights. I can't let the naysayers stop me from speaking my divine truth or be afraid to speak up. This new awareness helped me get through the harsh corporate environment.

It makes a major difference when you finally understand that we chose everything and all is perfect no matter what it looks like. A lot of peace and acceptance come with accepting this truth. Sometimes we forget when we are suffering. We allow it to consume us to the point of disconnecting from this truth, but even the disconnect is necessary.

I'm grateful for the friends who stood by my side and helped me remember who I truly am. A dear friend helped me realize that moving to this new state was a choice. This choice led me to face my fears and heal the residue of my past. I needed to face my deepest fears and heal them to set myself free. The state I moved to triggered everything needed in order to recognize what required attention, love and healing. With the new depth of courage I was building, I was tapping into a level of confidence that I could not reach while living in paradise. I began to feel more confidence in the authenticity of who I truly am, which I could carry with me anywhere. I realized paradise had prepared me to have the strength to endure what I was going to live through in the new state. The previous years prepared me, allowing me to grow spiritually, and strengthened me emotionally in order to face everything holding me back from my divine mission and destiny.

It took a year and a half for me to begin to see the blessing in disguise. I began to remember there is no right or wrong. All is divinely orchestrated. It was all part of my divine destiny. Now I realize I was manifesting my heart's desire the entire time. I asked the universe to remove all the blocks that held me back from my heart's desire. I just didn't expect it to be this way. I realize now that this work couldn't be done anywhere else. I had to come back to my roots to where it all began--all my trauma and fear. As I continue to release and heal my past, my courageous heart began to emerge.

On my healing journey I was led to a new healing modality that assisted me in releasing the past. I met this amazing couple who became a big role in helping me let go of the past trauma that was blocking my abundant life. At the time one of my dearest friends had just published her book, "How I Stopped My Slow Suicide." In her book she shares her ten-year painful journey living with severe gastrointestinal issues. She also shares how she overcame this pain. I began to use her tools and soon after I manifested healing modalities that took the pain away.

This couple introduced me to Biodecoding. I was fascinated how this healing modality worked on healing ancestral energy, patterns, and cycles. We carry the torch of unhealed or unresolved issues from family members. In Biodecoding you get the opportunity to heal the family tree. Everything you carry from your parents, grandparents, aunts, uncles, and cousins--even family members you never met--can be healed and released. After only a few sessions I noticed a major shift in my life. I was suffering with severe Irritable Bowel Syndrome. I struggled with this in my teen and early twenties but then had no issues with my colon until I moved home. I was seeing different doctors who were trying to get my health under control, but it only became worse. I was rushed to the hospital in severe pain and I couldn't understand why this was surfacing. I sent love and gratitude to the pain. I knew it was trying to communicate with me. My colon was holding on to all the emotions of the traumatic experiences I had recently lived. I needed to release those emotions in order for the pain to subside and my colon to work properly.

I started off with their therapeutic massage that focused on the colon area along with several Biodecoding sessions. I began to feel the release and relief immediately. My colon worked properly again and the pain left. Abundance surfaced again and money flowed back into my life. I was manifesting with great ease. Unexpected opportunities emerged and there were more miracles in my life. As I was letting go of my past, a wave of blessings followed. Life changed and moved in the direction that aligned with my heart's desires. If you are interested in healing your family tree and letting go of the past, I recommend you seek additional information at luzreikiwellness.com (English) or www. luzreiki.net (Spanish).

Today I live with the excitement of what the future has in store for me, and I also live in the present. I stay mindful of all that I have learned and of the blessing in the lessons. I'm excited to discover how much more is in store for me. Life may not turn out the way you want or expect; however, it can turn out better than you ever dreamed possible! If you can find it inside yourself to accept any painful experience as an opportunity to learn, grow, and evolve, you'll be able to find peace in the storm. When you believe everything is perfect, no matter what it looks like, you will accept everything as an opportunity to reach levels inside yourself you wouldn't have otherwise. There is a beautiful gift in the act of surrender. It allows you to flow in the direction of your soul's purpose and that's when miracles happen.

My aunt was one of the greatest examples in my life in showing me the power of faith, positive attitude and hope. She was diagnosed with terminal cancer at the age of twenty-four. She underwent chemotherapy and brain surgery; however, the cancer was in its aggressive stage and she was given six months to live. Her unshakable faith kept her alive for twenty years. Those years were very difficult and painful. She experienced several treatments, hospitalizations and paralysis. Even though she couldn't walk, and had to be in bed all day, she never lost her positive spirit. She always had a smile on her face, no matter how much pain she was experiencing. People visited hoping to inspire her, but it was she who inspired others.

I remember my aunt telling me in confidence she had moments when she felt like dying. It was difficult for her to see us all living our lives while she had to lay bedridden and watch, but that didn't stop her from smiling and shining her light on all who visited. I watched her deteriorate through the years. She lost her beauty and her mind. I would sit for hours and watch her in agony. It was her strength, faith, perseverance, and resilience that kept her alive. She inspired me to get through my own pain with a smile on my face.

It's been over ten years since her passing and my aunt continues to inspire me. Doctors never understood how she lived that long, but we knew she lived to teach us what faith and miracles really are. If you're living through an illness, don't lose hope in your recovery. Have faith in God's power. See your illness as a gift and an opportunity to learn and inspire others in the process. Only God knows your expiration date. Try to find the blessing in your illness, and don't waste precious time focusing on your pain. See how this disease can become an inspiration for others, watch the healing, and the peace will come over you. If you can apply the principle of finding those lessons it will lead you to self- improvement, allowing you to create what you want, in turn creating blessings in your life. Most crucial is acceptance. If we can accept that everything happens for a divine reason and for our growth, we'll find peace. I always believe something good comes out of whatever it is I'm experiencing. Even though I don't see it in the moment, I know I will learn something important about myself. I remember when my son was experiencing his manic episode he said, "Mom, I know this looks bad, but it's not. This is a process of elimination." I can see what that meant now. He was shedding the old parts of himself that no longer served him. His manic episode was truly a blessing in disguise. I can see how much he has changed and grown for the better. I recognize how each hospitalization was a representation of his soul's evolution. I used to fear those times and now I am grateful for them.

BLESSING IN THE PAIN

What was the most painful experience in your life?

_____

_____

_____

_____

_____

What did this experience teach you about yourself and others?

_____

_____

_____

_____

_____

What blessing did you discover through your pain?

_____

_____

_____

_____

_____

Where did that pain lead you?

_____

_____

_____

_____

_____

What are you doing different now due to that experience?

_____
_____
_____
_____
_____
_____

How has it changed your life for the better?

_____
_____
_____
_____
_____

How can your experience help others?

_____
_____
_____
_____
_____

"Life comes with hardships, losses and stress, but it also comes with love, joy, peace and happiness. Our life is truly a precious gift. Choose to live it with gratitude, hope and faith no matter what your experience is."

Key 4

Magical Perspective

O UR VIEW OF life's experiences can highly affect how we feel. If you see things in a negative light, you'll feel pain. However, if you choose to see things in a positive light, you'll feel peace. If you choose to see the world as a place of learning, goodness, support, and abundance, it will help you navigate through the storms of life with greater ease and peace. If you see pain as an opportunity for growth and learning you will not carry regrets and judgments of your life's journey. Accepting that everything is perfect, no matter what it looks like, keeps the soul at peace. Seeing hardships as stepping stones that lead you to your heart's desire versus seeing them as painful experiences that you wish never happened, help you remain grateful for each experience.

These painful experiences can create a false belief system that will attract everything we don't want. This negative belief system is created by experiencing losses, rejection, abandonment, the death of a loved one, or any form of abuse (physical, emotional, mental or bullying). Everything we experience sends a message to our subconscious. The subconscious part of our mind is running the show. It dictates the people and events who will show up in our lives. Automatically the subconscious creates false beliefs such as:

- I'm not good enough.
- I'm not worthy or deserving.
- I'm not lovable.
- I'm a failure.
- I'm stupid.

These false beliefs can trigger emotions, such as:

- Sadness
- Depression
- Helplessness
- Lack of faith
- Lack of motivation
- Lack of self-worth
- Lack of self-love

These negative emotions are what keep us in the dark. As long as we are feeling and thinking in a negative way, we will continue to attract people, places, and situations that keep us feeling this way. We then allow these false beliefs to take control of our lives. We find ourselves experiencing negative situations and attracting negative people which keeps alive our false belief system. However, when we change those false beliefs and we begin to see life for what it really is, understanding we are responsible for the creation of our lives, we change our lives.

At birth our mind was open to receive any and all information. The information that was programmed in our mind determined how we see ourselves and our life experiences. Our minds are like computers filled with files downloaded since infancy. We also carry our book of life, which is our entire library of all our past lifetimes. We arrive with wounds we hadn't healed in the past and with karmic debt. If we didn't resolve something in a past life, we come to heal. Also, we carry our ancestral energy that we've inherited, which is stored in our DNA.

If our current or past life experiences were based on hardships, lack of love, lack of attention, put downs, and let downs, we'll have very poor self-esteem. We will automatically develop feelings of not being good enough, worthy and lovable. We'll naturally believe that life is hard, painful and unhappy. Life will seem hopeless, and we will believe that nothing good will ever happen to us (or if it does, it won't last long and that we'll never find happiness).

However, if our current or past life experiences are based on happy and healthy experiences full of success, achievements, and love, then we're programmed to naturally believe that life is good, fun and easy. If we were raised receiving love, compassion, and compliments we would naturally have healthy self-esteem and feel lovable. However, no one is immune to pain. As long as we are living our human experience eventually challenges, losses, and suffering will show up in our lives. Most of our life experiences tend to be difficult and full of suffering, but no matter how dysfunctional and painful your life has been until now, it doesn't have to be this way forever. You have the power to change your belief system and create a happy and healthy life.

I have proven through my own journey that we have the power within ourselves to go as far as to even change our DNA. Also, what we didn't heal or overcome in our past lives, we are given the opportunity to conquer now. Sometimes we don't understand why we have certain issues and we fail to explore the possibility of past life trauma or karma.

In order to accomplish this we must clear our subconscious mind and change its belief system. We'll need to dig deep in our subconscious, and delete those negative programs and replace them with positive ones. Once we do that, we'll be able to have a different view of ourselves, others, and our life. Our perspective about ourselves and life will dramatically change.

The way to do that is by first recognizing what keeps showing up in our life. Our outer world is a reflection of our inner world. If the same situations keep surfacing, the lesson hasn't been learned and the subconscious keeps ruling our life. No matter what the conscious mind thinks and believes, it doesn't really matter if the subconscious is not in agreement. The key is getting the subconscious in agreement with the conscious. Then we'll start attracting what our heart truly desires. It is not an easy task and there isn't only one way to accomplish this. It's not something that can be fixed overnight. However, I will help you identify what's currently ruling your life through the subconscious and will provide you with information that can lead you to getting your mind to align with your heart's desires.

PROGRAMMING

What is currently showing up in your life?

_____

_____

_____

_____

_____

Which areas in your life are you not happy with?

_____

_____

_____

_____

_____

What patterns do you keep repeating?

_____

_____

_____

_____

_____

What emotions do these painful experiences trigger?

_____

_____

_____

_____

_____

What negative thoughts do you have about the areas in your life that are not working out for you?

For example: If you're struggling with money your false belief can be "Money is hard to get." If you struggle with relationships, your false belief can be "I'm not lovable or good enough." If it's your career or job, then your false belief can be "My dream career or job is not possible to achieve, because I'm not talented."

_____

_____

_____

_____

_____

When do you believe this false belief could have been created?

For example: Did your parents have to work really hard for money just to make ends meet? Did you not receive love and praise as a child? Did you grow up surrounded by family and friends who have careers or jobs they hate?

_____

_____

_____

_____

_____

At what point in your life could these false beliefs have been created?

_____

_____

_____

_____

_____

How can you shift these false beliefs to a positive belief?

_____

_____

_____

_____

_____

The moment we are able to recognize what's in our subconscious mind, we will have the ability to change our programming by deleting any negativity and replacing it with a positive belief system. Keep in mind it will not be an instant fix. It took years to program your mind to think negatively, and it will take some time to program it to think positively. However, the moment we can see what's in the subconscious we'll be able to immediately recognize why we're attracting what we don't want. This awareness will help us stop ourselves from allowing people and situations into our life that will bring us pain. Also, the moment we see the positive in the situation we will feel instant peace.

As we work on deleting false beliefs and replacing them with positive beliefs we will notice dramatic changes in our outer world. We will start attracting more of what we want versus what we don't. If we're not feeling good about ourselves, we will attract people and situations that will keep us feeling that way. On the other hand, if we feel great about ourselves we will attract people and situations that support how good we feel. Our view of ourselves is what truly matters. Once we understand the importance of having a positive view of ourselves, not only will we create the life we want, we'll also find our bliss. A quick indicator of our thought process is our emotions. Our emotions are a reflection of our thoughts. If we're feeling good, then our thoughts will reflect that, versus if we're feeling sad, this emotion is an indicator that our thoughts need shifting.

By now you have identified what your false beliefs are. That is the biggest battle. They are now in the conscious, which will allow you to replace them with positive thoughts. One of the most powerful affirmations starts with "I am." The more the subconscious hears "I am," it believes it is.

Here are a few examples:

OLD BELIEF: I am always broke.
NEW BELIEF: I am full of abundance.

OLD BELIEF: I am not lovable or good enough.
NEW BELIEF: I am lovable and good enough.

OLD BELIEF: I am not worthy.
NEW BELIEF: I am worthy.

OLD BELIEF: I am destined to a career/job I hate.
NEW BELIEF: I am successful in doing what I love.

OLD BELIEF: I am always sick.
NEW BELIEF: I am healthy and feel great.

The more you speak to the subconscious with the "I am" affirmation, the more you will be amazed at what you will attract. Also, these affirmations will shift you energetically and will create feelings of positivity and hope. As much as I believe in the power of the I am, I also believe in seeking spiritual healers to help clear the subconscious. A spiritual healer can tap into past lives that can be affecting you in this lifetime and help heal them. If there are any ancestral connections that were passed to you genetically they can help you identify them and clear those attachments. Biodecoding is an amazing healing modality that I use to help people heal family programs, illnesses, cycles, patterns, limiting beliefs, and anything that is blocking abundance/success. When I began using this healing modality I attracted abundance into my life again almost immediately.

As a spiritual healer and facilitator, I can connect to the angels for guidance and healing not only for myself, but for others. When I access a client's Akashic Records it allows me to see what needs to be cleared and healed, such as: past life and current life trauma, ancestral energy, negative belief systems, and everything that is blocking the person from their heart's desire. The angels guide me through the session with clear direction and instructions of what the person needs. I also use Integrated Energy Therapy to pull out trauma from the person's energy field. As we experience traumatic events, these emotions are stored in our energy fields. However, through IET, I clear the energy in the person's body which leads to clearing the path for positive situations to manifest.

As you work on clearing your subconscious, you will notice your negative thoughts and negative perspective shift to a more positive state. You'll see more of the good in your life and less of the unsatisfying parts. On a rainy day, it's human nature to focus on the clouds and not on the blossoming flowers. We all have something in our life that is good. We just need to stop and take a closer look.

Look around you; you will be amazed at what you see. We take so much for granted because we focus on the parts of our lives that are hard or unfulfilled.

But if we really stop to look at what we have—we are truly blessed. Others would only dream to have what we take for granted.

- The homeless person wishes to have that little house you wish were bigger.
- That mother who lost her son would do anything to deal with your defiant child.
- The father who cannot feed his three kids would love to go to the job you hate.

- The woman riding her bike ten miles to work wishes to have the car you want to trade in.
- That lonely woman would love the man who forgets to take out the garbage or doesn't pick up after himself.
- That orphan child wouldn't mind the mother who makes him clean his dirty room.
- The physically challenged adolescent would love to climb the flight of stairs you dread.
- The woman in the hospital dying of cancer wishes to rush home after work to cook her family a meal.

You see, it's all in how we look at things.

If we examine our lives with the right perspective and focus on the blessings, we will be filled with gratitude. To focus on what we have and not on what we don't – that is the best way to live.

In the end, the biggest joy and blessing is love. If you look hard enough, you'll be amazed at how much love surrounds you and how much you truly have. What you have today you will miss someday. Make it a point today to focus on what you have and not on what you have yet to achieve. Shifting your perspective will allow you to find your bliss no matter what your life's circumstances are.

When we're able to be grateful for what we have, we open the door for more good to enter. Plus we find ourselves feeling good about our life. Wouldn't you rather feel good about what you have now, versus feeling down about what you have yet to achieve? I highly recommend a gratitude journal to find the good in your daily life. After my morning meditation, I write in my journal. I find my day goes smoother and I feel more peace. I'm able to shift quickly any negative situations or thoughts that may surface throughout the day. Starting your day on a positive note will contribute to experiencing a positive day. You'll be able to handle the challenges that may arise with greater ease.

I was blessed to come across a great therapist who had the gift of shifting distorted perspectives to what I call magical perspective. I would go to her with a dark picture of my experience and she would send me home with an entirely different picture. She helped me see the beauty in the experiences I was currently living. This helped me release the heavy burden of my distorted perspective that was keeping me in the dark and in a state of suffering. With her help my life began to change dramatically for the better.

There will be things in life that we have no control over, but we do have control over our reactions to them. We can choose to react peacefully or in a panic. The situation won't change, what will change is how we feel about it. That in itself changes how we see or experience the situation. The heaviness we carry is the weight of our perspective. The moment we shift our perspective, we shift the situation. You'll notice how the weight is immediately lifted and you will experience a deep sense of relief.

Key 5

Mastering Self-love

THE JOURNEY TOWARDS self-love is not for the weary as you will have to face the darkest parts of your shadow self and learn to love those parts. Every painful experience in our lives is an opportunity to bring us back to love. Not everyone is meant to master self-love, but for those who are meant to, it can be quite challenging and unique. You will have to delve deep into your soul and see the truth in the wounds that are keeping you from the love within. You will have to feel the pain in its rawness. You will have to let go of judgments of the self and embrace the parts you once ignored. Most of us struggle with loving ourselves and feeling good enough, no matter what our childhood was like. I grew up in a dysfunctional environment and my sons grew up in a healthy home. Regardless of our upbringing we still have to experience the journey towards self-love. I believed if I gave my sons a happy childhood they wouldn't have to go through the inner painful journey towards self-love. As they became teenagers and young adults, I learned they also had their own journey and contracts to honor and I had to learn to accept and find peace with their painful journeys. They also came with past lives that needed healing and experienced traumatic events they needed to heal. Even though they grew up hearing how great and special they are, they still struggle with self-esteem issues. They are learning how to love themselves. I now know it's what we came to do when we chose to incarnate to this planet.

However, if we have lived through abuse, bullying, neglect, or abandonment of any kind, our struggle is a lot greater. It's easy to fall into the belief system that we are not lovable if someone abandons us, puts us down, doesn't take care of us, or beats us down physically, emotionally, and mentally. We unconsciously start treating ourselves in the same way others have treated us. Then we wonder why we continue to relive what we don't want. One of my biggest and most valuable lessons was learning I couldn't truly love others unconditionally until I learned to love myself unconditionally. The only way to build self-worth is through self-love, but first we must identify if we are practicing self-love.

Signs of a lack of self-love include:

- Putting yourself down and beating yourself up for your mistakes.
- Always giving to others and not giving to yourself.
- Not taking care of your mind, body, and soul.
- Not doing the things you love.
- Always pleasing others and putting yourself last.
- Making excuses as to why you can't do nice things for yourself.
- Allowing others to mistreat you.
- Being a perfectionist.

On the other hand when you love yourself, you:

- Make yourself a priority.
- Forgive yourself and others.

- Find ways to do things for yourself that bring you joy.
- Give to yourself first before you give to others.
- Praise yourself for the beautiful person you are.
- Point out the great parts of your body that are beautiful.
- Say nice things to yourself and accept compliments.
- Believe you are perfect just the way you are.

Loving ourselves is a big part of achieving happiness. It is the gateway to self-acceptance. As we learn to accept all of the parts of ourselves, imperfections and all, we then achieve internal peace. This inner peace leads us to tapping into joy. No outer accomplishments or material things will make you happy. Happiness truly is an inside job.

When we love ourselves we build our self-worth. As we see and feel our worth, we begin to feel enough. Feeling enough eliminates the blocks that keep abundance from manifesting into our lives. As long as we continue to feel that we are not enough, we will block ourselves from manifesting the desires of our heart. We will attract what we believe--that we are not deserving. We will be sending that message out to the universe and the universe will respond with lack. However, if you know and feel that you are enough, and what you desire is part of your soul's contract and divine plan, the universe will respond with your heart's desire.

When we don't feel good enough, we will constantly attract people and situations that keep us feeling that way about ourselves. We will continue to repeat the same patterns which will result in the same situations over and over again. We'll live in a vicious cycle with no end. This is why it's extremely important to build our self-worth. It's the only way we will be able to create the life we truly desire. As we master self-love, we'll start to attract people who will love us, respect us, value us, and see us as the lovable person we are. We'll begin to feel aligned and centered. This inner balance will guide us to our life's purpose. Discovering our life's purpose can lead us to the job that will bring us joy. We'll also attract a partner who loves him/herself and together create a healthy relationship. As we become whole we will attract a partner who is also whole. This will also automatically bring in financial abundance because energetically we feel deserving. Once we achieve and master feeling good enough, we will no longer accept anything or anyone who keeps us from our inner bliss.

One of the ways to begin our self-love journey is through healing our inner child. Loving our inner child and giving him/her the attention needed can be incredibly healing. As children we picture ourselves becoming anything we want. When we play we believe we are teachers, doctors, nurses, lawyers, athletes, counselors, actors, singers, authors, firefighters, police officers, and anything that interests us. We play these roles with our friends as if we were already living them. We feel that everything and anything is possible. Children don't question not having the funds or being good enough. There is that assurance that the dream will come to life. We don't see obstacles or road bumps; all we see is the possibility. Along the way we lose that belief system. Life experiences rob us of that innocence, and our inner child becomes wounded. The inner child no longer believes he or she is good enough or capable of achieving these dreams. It begins to feel neglected and abandoned by us when we don't practice self-love. The more love you give to your inner child, the more it heals.

When I was a child I used to play house, and I believed I had a great husband with great children. I also had a chalkboard and taught my big group of students. I knew I was a great wife, mother, and teacher. I didn't think for once that I wouldn't have what I knew I deserved. It was through trauma that my beliefs changed. I no longer had the confidence in myself and no longer felt deserving of what I once thought I could have. My inner child was crushed by this realization. Her innocence was lost, her dreams vanished, and her self-esteem crushed. There began my painful journey full of devastation. When I began to heal her, I was able to believe in my dreams being a reality as well as how deserving I am.

One of the most effective healing tools I used to heal my inner child was a stuffed animal. I had a teddy bear my brother had given me as a gift. I dressed it up as a girl and used her as my inner child. I slept with her, held her while watching TV, talked to her, and hugged her constantly. The healing power, which I felt immediately, amazed me. Some of you may be thinking this concept is nuts, but I promise you: it works. When I felt sad, I would ask her why and she would answer. She helped me discover what was in my subconscious that kept me from feeling self-love. There were moments I would ask my inner child what it needed to feel loved, and I would allow the answer to guide me. Every time I needed to feed my inner child I would grab my teddy bear and find immediate inner love.

For those of you who are not comfortable with this concept, there is still hope. I have other tools I will share with you that will heal your inner child. Some of my clients have used a doll and that's been as effective as a teddy bear. Bonding with your inner child through love and attention helps him/her feel he/she is enough. You begin to feel important, loved, and believe you deserve all that is good. If this concept doesn't work for you, I recommend you do the following exercise:

Find a quiet space where you will not be interrupted. Close your eyes and see yourself as a child in front of you. Speak these words to the child: "I love you and I'm here for you. I will not leave you or

abandon you. You are beautiful, special, loveable, and good enough.
Tell me what I need to do to help you feel loved."

Listen to the answer and give your inner child exactly what it's asking for (i.e. encouragement, love, attention, hugs, etc.) Your inner child is craving love and attention. You will be amazed how much of a difference it will make in yourself and in your life loving your inner child. It's your core being that you're truly loving. Tapping in to that deep part of yourself and feeding it the love and attention it needs can heal very deep-rooted wounds. Wounds that were created in this lifetime and those that were never healed in past lives.

Another important factor in loving ourselves is our self-talk. It's important for us to treat ourselves as we would our best friend. Our self-talk is an indicator of how we are treating ourselves. If we're saying negative things to ourselves, we are not practicing self-love. If we make a mistake and beat ourselves up instead of forgiving ourselves, then we're not being a best friend to ourselves. Self-love requires us to be kind, loving, considerate, patient, understanding, and non- judgmental with ourselves. Watch your self-talk and keep in mind that you hurt your inner child when you criticize yourself. In the moment you catch yourself putting yourself down, shift immediately and think something positive. Focus on the good qualities and attributes about yourself. Point out the things you love about yourself and send love to the things you don't. Find the beauty in your imperfections. We all have insecurities; it's how we deal with them that makes the difference.

Many of us are not happy with our bodies. We tend to think we're not good enough if we don't have perfect bodies and that we are not lovable or desirable to a potential romantic partner because of our flaws. Women especially carry this insecurity because society has promoted the idea of bikini bodies being most desirable to men. If we are over-weight, have stretch marks or are not proportional, we believe a man won't want us. Some women struggle with feeling too old. They think after a certain age no man will want them. Some even believe that men only want younger women. These false beliefs are what will keep men away. As soon as they see our lack of self-worth we become unattractive. However, if we embrace our imperfect body and focus on the parts that are beautiful, we become desirable. Men seek confidence more than anything. They can have a woman with a perfect body, but if she lacks self-worth, self-love, and confidence she becomes unattractive. On the other hand, a woman who has an imperfect body, yet has self-worth, self-love, and confidence, becomes extremely beautiful and desirable. These are the women men adore and want to marry. Think about it—there are people in wheel chairs, burn victims, or are deformed or even simply overweight, who are adored by great partners—proving that what our body looks like has nothing to do with being lovable and desirable. It's who we are at the core that makes us attractive.

Some of us base our worth on our outer achievements. We live in a world where titles, degrees, status, looks, and wealth are looked at as the definition of success. However, true success lies in mastering self-love which leads to happiness. When we die it doesn't matter what our outer accomplishments were, what matters is the people who loved us enough to be at our side as we take our last breath.

I personally know many people that have college degrees yet are not successful in their professional life. But I also know many people without college degrees, including myself, who are successful. When I was sixteen I decided to leave my dysfunctional home and live on my own. I tried to stay in high school and work to support myself, however that became almost impossible. I decided to drop out of high school and work a full-time job. A family from the church I was attending rented me a room and I found a job as a legal assistant at a well-known law firm. Every time I tried to go back to school there were big obstacles that didn't allow me that opportunity. Then I married and had children. That became my priority and school took a back seat. I still wanted to finish school and get my degree in psychology. However, every time I tried, it didn't work out. I suffered very low self-esteem for years as I was defining my worth around a diploma and degree. Interesting enough, I was always able to find really great job opportunities. I worked with top executives most of my life and even had my own businesses. I was never rich, but lived very comfortable. Most of my life my salary was more than people I knew with bachelor's degrees. I'm not in any way encouraging people to not graduate high school or go to college, but it's not for everyone. It's not everyone's journey. It definitely wasn't mine. I discovered that my passion was coaching, writing, and speaking. I pursued my passion and trained for what I loved. I trained with very successful authors, speakers, and writers. I may not have a degree, but I have all the certifications for my training. My path didn't require a degree and I see that now. I no longer base my worth on school or credentials. My worth comes from just being me. I encourage everyone to discover your passion and do whatever it takes to follow it. If it requires a degree, then that's your journey, but if it doesn't, then that's great too.

A degree doesn't determine your success. It's what you do with the degree. If you research the background of entrepreneur millionaires, most of them don't have any type of degrees; some haven't even graduated high school. Their success is not based on their intelligence. Their drive, determination, perseverance, positive, and deserving attitude are what sets them apart. They don't have limiting beliefs about themselves or what they can accomplish. They have a vision for their lives and they believe in creating that vision. They follow their passion and do whatever it takes to achieve it regardless of the setbacks, disappointments, and trial and error. No degree can give them the qualities it takes to achieve their dream. The ultimate goal: happiness. Do what makes you happy.

In reality there are no limits to what we all can achieve. Nothing stops us but ourselves. It's our limiting belief system that keeps us stuck in life. Some of us believe we are not smart enough. Personally I struggled with this my entire life. Having a stepfather who called me stupid all the time didn't help. Also, I have a unique way of learning that the school system didn't support. I struggled in school and that contributed to believing I wasn't intelligent. It was a long journey for me to discover that I was smart in my own way. I learned we are all good at something. We all have different gifts, talents, and abilities. Once we discover what those are, we can then begin to believe that we are brilliant. This will contribute to our self-love.

Most of the time we don't see ourselves as others see us. We tend to be our own worst critic. One of the exercises that helped me shift my view of self was seeing others' view of me. I had my family and friends compile a list of positive qualities they loved about me. As I looked over the list, I was surprised to see things they saw in me that I never would have seen in myself. This was a true eye-opener. I recommend you do the same. Ask your loved ones to compose a list of all the positive qualities they love about you. In the meantime, compose one of yourself describing your positive attributes.

Once you have everyone's list, place the lists in an area where you can see them every day. Also write on a Post-It the qualities about yourself that you need constant reminders of. Place those notes in different areas of your house, car, or workspace. When you find yourself thinking or feeling anything negative about yourself, read your list and remind yourself of all the greatness in you. You'll be amazed at how this simple exercise can really help you change the way you see yourself.

Create another list as well: of all the things you love to do and that bring you joy. On a daily basis select at least three things from that list and do them. Starting your day with a gratitude journal will help you feel good about yourself and your life. The key is to recognize what feels good to you—and then make it a daily practice. Two of the most helpful things for me have been meditation and prayer. Through meditation I'm able to quiet the noise in my mind and fully connect to my soul. Here I find my balance, peace, and answers. I'm able to recognize what's in my subconscious, which leads to the shifts that are necessary for my growth.

There are many different ways to achieve self-love, and you need to do what feels right to you. What works for you may not work for someone else. Once you find a healthy way that helps you feel good about yourself, commit to practice it on a daily basis. It takes practice, but the more you do it, you'll notice how it becomes your default.

Playing is also an effective way of healing your inner child and mastering self-love. Doing things that are fun are important. It feeds the inner child love, attention, and feelings of importance. Play in the park. Ride carousels and horses. Play games with family and friends. Go ride go-carts with some friends. Watch movies and dance. Have family or friends over for a barbecue. These are just some examples of loving your inner child and giving him/her the attention he/she needs. Give it a try! You'll be surprised how good you feel afterwards. Here are some additional exercises you can do that will help you master self-love.

"If you are searching for love begin with loving yourself and watch how love will naturally find you."

SELF-LOVE PRACTICES

What three things can I do today that bring me joy?

For example: (read an uplifting quote or article; take a bubble bath; drink warm tea; journal/write; meditate; pray; exercise; eat healthy; spend time with positive people; work on a hobby; compliment yourself, etc.)

1)_____

2)_____

3)_____

I celebrate:_____

_____

I deserve:_____

_____

I am worthy of:_____

_____

I am grateful for (list at least 10):

1)_____

2)_____

3)_____

4)_____

5)_____

6)_____

7)_____

8)_____

9)_____

10)_____

I appreciate _____about myself.

I appreciate _____about my body.

I appreciate _____about my family.

I appreciate _____about my friend/friends.

I appreciate _____about my work.

I appreciate _____about my life.

POSITIVE CHANGES

- Surround yourself with positive people who love and support you.
- Let go of anyone or anything that brings you down.
- Release all negativity around you.
- Be part of a community via online or in your neighborhood that is like- minded.
- Be mindful of your self-talk.

- Invest time and energy in programs/mentors/teachers and coaches.
- Write a letter from God/Higher Power/Spirit. Let Him speak to you and share with you how He sees you and feels about you.
- Write a letter to God/Higher Power/Spirit expressing your feelings towards Him.

DAILY AFFIRMATIONS

I am a worthy of my heart's desires.
I am a lovable being.
I am whole.

I am the experience of joy.
I am healthy.
I am one with God.
I am loved.
I am beautiful.
I am smart.
I am talented.

I am more than enough.
I am abundant.
I am debt free.

I am financially free.
I am strong.
I am positive.

I am full of peace.

I am grateful for the blessings in my life.
I am balance.
I am energy.

I am a powerful creator.
I am unique.
I am special.

I am 100% responsible for my own happiness.

We might find it challenging at first to make these practices part of our daily life. But self-love requires us to be gentle with ourselves. Keep in mind that it will take time to master self-love, but it will be worth the effort. Make yourself a priority and watch how the quality of your life expands. When you are able to give to yourself, you are then equipped to give to others. The giving will come from a place of joy, not obligation. You will feel whole and won't need to be filled by others. You will no longer depend on others for approval or happiness. Your soul will be filled with everything it needs to feel peace and joy.

"When we love and accept ourselves for who we truly are, we can then feel the serenity in our soul, and experience the true meaning of unconditional love."

Another practice that can contribute to mastering self-love, is to love others unconditionally. Loving others can be quite difficult, especially when all we can see are their flaws. Yet there is great peace in choosing to love others unconditionally. It's not only a gift to others, but a gift to yourself. How do we love someone who we do not consider a good person or someone who has hurt us? Well, we start by seeing the good in him or her. Everyone has something good inside. As imperfect human beings, we tend to focus on the negative traits of others, yet if we make a conscious choice to focus on the good in others it becomes easier to love them.

My stepfather is a man who has never been faithful to any woman, has gone to jail for drug trafficking, is an arsonist, steals from the poor, and is abusive and mean. Yet I have love in my heart for him and I wish him well. It sounds crazy, but I see him as a man with a lot of trauma that was never addressed. His mother abandoned him, and he's constantly struggling with the rejection from the people he loves. He has never received love, compassion, and understanding. Deep down is a troubled soul, only wanting to be loved and accepted. A lot of who I am today, I owe to him. He taught me to be strong, courageous, responsible, a hard worker, and clean, and to go after my dreams. I choose to focus on the great things I learned from him and not on the hurt he caused others or me.

Choose someone in your life whom you can't seem to find it in your heart to love. List all the bad things you see in him/her.

_____

_____

_____

_____

_____

Now think of something good you see in him/her. Keep in mind that everyone has something good in him or her.

_____

_____

_____

_____

_____

From now on when you think of this person and start thinking of all the reasons why you can't love him/her, remind yourself of that one thing you were able to find and focus on it. Little by little you'll find yourself seeing the person in a different light: as a troubled human being doing the best he/she can with what he/she knows. Then you'll notice how your heart starts to feel compassion and surprisingly love. When we change our view we change our feelings.

Conclusion

THESE FIVE KEYS have helped me throughout the most difficult and painful times in my life. They have helped me tap into my center creating peace, and joy in all the storms that come my way.

Life is all about ups and downs. However, if we practice these tools through those difficult and painful times, we can navigate through them with grace. The more we practice staying in touch with our inner peace, the easier it will be to access in difficult times. Believe that every experience is a lesson, leading you to your spiritual growth. When we learn to embrace hardships, life becomes a lot sweeter.

In life we can be hit with rocks so big, leaving us bruises and scars so deep, that one can barely get up. With every hit, one falls, but God always catches us. He pulls those rocks off us, and helps us, by walking with us hand in hand.

Life will be filled with tests and hardships. I call them storms— storms that can consume so much of our being, storms that leave us holding on with all our might, struggling not to let go, struggling to survive.

Some of us get hit harder than others, but the strong ones who live through these storms, are the ones who come out victorious. There is an amazing feeling that comes with the victory of strength, perseverance, determination, and most of all faith. With each fall, with each hit, a lesson is learned. With each lesson comes growth. With growth comes maturity. We learn not to regret the hardship, but to be thankful for it, and the growth that we experience.

We must not look back at our past mistakes with regret. What seems as a mistake is merely an opportunity to learn something. We need to accept those mistakes as part of our journey for a better future. We must embrace those experiences, and allow them to mold us into the best we can be. No one knows what life will bring. Each day will come with its own challenges, but we must be strong, believing that God will get us through. With God all things are possible!

Resources

Akashic/IET/Life Coaching : www.myakashichealing.com
Transcendental Meditation: www.tm.org
Reiki/Biodecoding/Massage Therapy: www.luzreikiwellness.com (English)
or www.luzreiki.net (Spanish).
Deepak Chopra Meditation CD's: www.chopracentermeditation.com
Doreen Virtue: www.angeltherapy.com/angel-numbers

About the Author

YANIRA CRESPO IS a Life Coach, Spiritual Counselor, and Speaker. Her experience in helping others reaches back to childhood, when people would naturally gravitate to her for guidance. She recognized this as her life's purpose and has committed herself to helping others heal trauma and find inner peace. Her personal spiritual journey has given her a tremendous amount of experience overcoming adversity. For the past twenty years she has studied psychology and spirituality with top experts who helped heal her, and countless others.

Her intuitive clairvoyant ability combined with Integrated Energy Therapy (IET), accessing the Akashic Records, and Biodecoding helps her reach beyond a client's perception, and brings to light situations, thoughts, and ideas that have been overlooked. She is gifted with the ability to go deep into the subconscious, and help remove any blocks that are holding you back from living the life of your choosing. Many have experienced significant healing, transformation, peace, and joy in their lives with her help.

If you are interested in her healing and speaking services, please visit www.myakashichealing.com for additional information.

973 272-5936

Made in the USA
Middletown, DE
20 November 2016